Know your job rights!

First Printing, February 1976

0-87094-115-1
Library of Congress Catalog Card No. 75–28954
Printed in the United States of America

Know your job rights!

WESLEY M. WILSON

DOW JONES-IRWIN

ISBN
Libra
Printe

Preface

If the broad field of labor and employment law is made clearer, then this book has served a major purpose.

New labor laws have been passed so fast by congress and state legislatures, and decisions of courts, government agencies, and labor arbitrators have become so numerous, that few employees have had time to understand their rights. A labor law is not effective unless the persons to whom it applies have a working knowledge of the rights and obligations established under the law. Knowledge is power.

Employees, management, and union agents should find the format of this book helpful, because it looks at labor law from the point of view of an employee seeking a job, working on a job, and being laid-off or terminated.

Problems frequently faced by employees are explored. Typical employment benefits are analyzed.

There have been few sources of information available to employees desiring further knowledge of their rights. Employees desiring more information have had to dig out that information bit by bit from various publications, from personal experience, and from government agencies, unions, and employers. I have tried in this book to provide that information in language that is easy to understand.

Yakima, Washington
January 1976

WESLEY M. WILSON

v

Contents

complaint to your employer. Antidiscrimination laws:, *Prohibited practices. Religion. Business necessity.* How to discuss your job performance with your boss. Work rules: *The "common law of the shop."* Rights of veterans. Fringe benefits. Employee benefit plans: *Hospital insurance. Group life insurance. Prescription drug insurance. Vision care. Dental insurance. Prepaid legal services. Paid sick leave. Injuries and workman's compensation.* Social Security: *Supplemental security income. Medical insurance.* Pensions and retirement plans: *Individual retirement account. Self-employed persons. Profit sharing. Types of pension plans. Other provisions. Pension Reform Act. Rights of participants.* Federal income tax deductions for employees: *Home office. Records. Moving expenses. Non-taxable income. Sick pay.*

How a union is organized: *Organizing an "independent union." Getting signatures. The appropriate bargaining unit. Getting recognition from the employer.* National Labor Relations Board election procedure: *Petition form. NLRB dollar jurisdiction requirements. Decertification elections. Union security elections. An employer may petition for an election. What the NLRB will do with the petition. Agreements for an election. Hearing to determine if election should be directed. Decision of NLRB regional director. Election eligibility list. Election campaign propaganda and meetings. Voting in NLRB elections. Mail ballot elections. Challenged ballots and objections. Certification. If a union is recognized: Early negotiation procedure. Coverage of union contracts. Union security. Grievances. Arbitration.* Court enforcement of collective bargaining agreements. *Overtime. Union negotiation procedure. Lockouts. Settlements. Union fines for working during a strike. Duties of unions.*

part four
If an employee is laid off or termi-
nated   119

If an employee is laid off or terminated—whether or
not there is a union: *Unemployment insurance. Layoff
pay. Antidiscrimination laws. Discrimination versus
seniority.* If an employee is laid off or terminated—
where a union represents him: *Types of seniority.
Mergers or consolidations of employers. Discrimination by unions.*

part five
Summary of federal and state labor
and employment agencies and laws   135

NLRB and unfair labor practices: *Charge form. Rights
of employees.* Employer unfair labor practices: *Interference, restraint, or coercion. Unlawful assistance to
union. Discrimination. Protection of witnesses. Refusal
to bargain.* Union unfair labor practices: *Restraint
and coercion. Restraint and coercion of employer
representatives. Discrimination in employment. Hiring
halls. Refusal to bargain. Hot cargo. Forcing independent contractors. Secondary boycotts. Coercion to
force recognition. Jurisdictional disputes. Excessive
or discriminatory membership fees. Featherbedding.
Picketing for organization, recognition, or bargaining.
Injunctions. Unfair labor practice procedure. Remedies.* Summary of federal and state agencies: *Railway
Labor Act. Equal Employment Opportunities Commission. Occupational Safety and Health Review Commission. State laws.* The Landrum-Griffin Act (Labor-
Management Reporting and Disclosure Act of 1959).

part six
Appendices   167

Contents

part one

Getting a job

Applying for a job

If you are applying for a job, you should have a fair understanding as to what type of work you are qualified to do by reason of experience, training, education, and physical ability. It is also helpful if you know what type of work is available and whether you may be qualified to do that work.

One of the best sources of jobs is your state employment office in your city or a nearby city. You may go to the state employment office, fill out an application form, listing your experience, training and education, and you may be provided with free counselling service by a state employee. The interviewer can summarize for you the types of positions for which you may be qualified and can provide you with information as to other openings in nearby areas. The state employment office also has available information about employment needs throughout the United States.

State employment offices

1

Private employment agencies

Another source of information about jobs is a private employment agency. Some states permit an agency to charge a fee for registering with the agency. You will also be expected to sign a contract in which you agree that if you are "placed" in a job to which they refer you, you will pay a stated fee for their placement service. This fee varies from state to state, but it may be either a flat fee or it may be a percentage of the gross earnings from your job for a period of time. If you are accepted for the job and soon quit it or are terminated, you are probably legally liable to pay the stated amount of the fee. Sometimes interviewers in a private employment agency are quite helpful in contacting employers to place you in a good job. If there is a demand by employers for someone with your qualifications, some employers will pay the agency's fee. Be sure to ask if the employer will pay.

A private employment agency is required to post a bond with a state agency in nearly all states. Misrepresentation about a job is prohibited in most states, and the splitting of fees between the employment agency and an employer or sending an applicant to an employer who has not sent in an order for a job to be filled are unlawful in many states. You may contact your state's department of labor, or see a private attorney if you believe that you were treated unfairly by an employment agency.

Newspaper ads

Another source of information about jobs is the "want ads" in your local newspaper or the ads of a distant city newspaper. You are less

likely to be hired if you never contact that employer in person since other applicants will
probably go to that employer in person and ag-
gressively make known their desires for the job.

Some individuals are successful in finding
jobs, particularly those for unskilled or semi-
skilled work, by going in person near the opening time each morning, to the office of a particular employer. Ask who does the interviewing
and hiring—an employment interviewer, plant
superintendent, or other official. After a period
of time, the official will probably realize that
you are quite interested in working there and if
there is an opening for which you are reasonably
well qualified, you are likely to be the first
hired.

**Rustle your
own job**

In some industries such as construction, mari-
time, longshoring, and over-the-road trucking,
many employers have a collective bargaining
agreement with a union that provides that all
applicants for employment must be referred to
that employer by a hiring hall operated by a
union. This is called an exclusive hiring hall. If
the union is unable to provide qualified applicants within a stated period of time, such as 48
hours, the employer is usually permitted to hire
from any other source, called "off the bank." A
union that operates an exclusive hiring hall is
prohibited by federal labor law (the National
Labor Relations Act, as amended) from giving
preference to its members or in refusing to dispatch someone solely because he or she is not
a member of that union. However, a union is
permitted to determine that an applicant is quali-

**Union hiring
halls**

fied to perform the type of work involved before permitting him to register at the union hiring hall. If the work involved is that of a construction craftsman, for example, an individual can be required to pass an objective written or verbal or a performance test before being permitted to qualify to register on the "out of work list." If local building codes require that particular construction craftsmen have a license, such as an electricians license, or a plumbers license, then an individual may properly be required to obtain such a license before registering on the "out of work list." If a test is administered to determine whether an applicant is qualified to do the work, it must be fairly administered and be objective. The test may not be in violation of federal labor laws if the union agent administers the test, so long as the employers in the industry have helped develop the test or agree that it is a fair test of ability of someone to do that kind of work.

A union is permitted to give first choice in job referrals to individuals who have worked out of that hiring hall for a period of time such as several years. Thus, if the local area has a surplus of individuals looking for that kind of work, a newcomer will probably not be successful in being referred to a job by a union hiring hall.

Agricultural laborers

If you work in agriculture for a farm labor contractor, many states have a law that requires such contractors to register with a state agency, usually the department of labor. Contractors are usually required to have a license, post a surety bond, are prohibited from misrepresentation about a job, must have vehicle liability insurance, and must pay workers promptly with a statement of wages and hours worked. Violations of the state law should be reported to the state agency that administers it, usually the labor department.

Many states also regulate farm labor camps, and require fresh water facilities and sanitary toilets for workers. Housing must meet minimum standards. These laws are usually administered by the state department of public health or the state labor department.

Federal law requires that farm labor contractors who furnish or transport across state lines nine or more migrant farm workers in a year, register with the U.S. Department of Labor.

If you are applying for a skilled or professional or management position, you will probably find it helpful to prepare neatly typewritten copies of a personal résumé. This should be not more than three or four pages. It should state your name, address, phone number and a summary of your work experience with the dates, name of employer reference or who to contact there. Your experience should be listed in chronological order with the most recent job listed first. Some employers prefer that you state the reason for leaving. Your training and education should be listed, also in chronological order, with an emphasis upon training that would be helpful for the job for which you are applying. Some individuals list their hobbies or

Personal résumé

other interests as well as references (other than previous employers) on the résumé. The important thing is that the résumé be neat in appearance, easy to read, and not too long.

Job interviews   In preparing for a job interview, you should be neat and clean, wearing the same type of clothes which you would expect to wear on the job for which you are applying. It is not necessary that a man wear a coat and tie, for example, unless it would be normal clothing for a holder of the job. Obviously, you should not chew gum and you should be neat in appearance. If you have an appointment for a particular time, do not be late.

Antidiscrimination laws

Federal laws and laws in over half of the states prohibit an employer from discriminating against an applicant for many reasons. For example, the National Labor Relations Board (NLRB) rules that if an employer refuses to hire an individual solely because he is a member of a union, or a supporter of a union the employer does not like, the employer commits an unfair labor practice and may be ordered to hire the applicant with back pay. Likewise, the NLRB prohibits an employer from requiring that an individual be a member of a particular union before he is hired. Of course, if that employer has a collective bargaining agreement with a union and that contract has a "union security clause," a new employee may be required after a stated number of days to join that union in order to keep his job. See Part Three, below, for a discussion of this law. Nearly half of the states have a labor relations act patterned after the federal law; most of these state laws prohibit a requirement that a job applicant be a member of any union. About 19 states, mostly in the South, Midwest, and Southwest, have a "right to work law" which usually prohibits a requirement that a job applicant or any employee be a member of, or pay dues or fees to, any union.

The federal Civil Rights Act of 1964, administered in part by the Equal Employment Opportunities Commission (EEOC), prohibits discrimination in employment because of an individual's race, color, national origin, religion, or sex. The EEOC has issued regulations interpreting the law, and in decisions in particular cases has provided us with guidelines as to what types of discrimination are unlawful.

It applies to most employers with 15 or more employees, and to a labor union with 15 or more members if it is the bargaining representative of any employees. It also applies to private, federal, and to most state employment agencies or offices.

Procedure for charges

If you believe that you have been discriminated against because of your race, color, national origin, religion, or sex, you may file a written charge or complaint with the EEOC within 180 days after the alleged unlawful act occurred. If you wait more than 180 days it is probably too late. (See Appendix C for addresses of EEOC offices.) If you live in a state with a fair employment practices act you must also file a written charge with your state agency within 180 days after the alleged unlawful act occurred. The charge should name the employer, union, or other agency you believe violated the law; it should summarize what happened, with names and dates; and it should be signed and dated by you or your representative (such as a union) who files the charge for you. The EEOC will within ten days inform the party against whom you filed the charge that a charge was filed, but it will not give that party your name. The EEOC protects your right to file a charge without fear of retaliation by your employer, the union, or others because of filing a charge.

If you live in a state that does not have an "approved" law prohibiting the type of discrimination you believe occurred, the EEOC should notify you in writing by a "suit letter" if within 180 days after your charge was filed it has not completed its investigation or has not satisfactorily settled the case. You may take your "suit letter" from the EEOC to a private attorney to represent you in suing in federal district court. If you cannot find a private attorney who will represent you for an amount you can afford, you may contact the federal district court in your area and ask that the court appoint an attorney to represent you. If you are planning to sue, you must do so within 90 days after receiving the EEOC's "suit letter"; if you wait it is probably too late.

If you live in a state with a fair employment practice law prohibiting the type of discrimination you believe occurred, you must file a charge with your state agency within 180 days after the alleged unfair act occurred, or you may be too late. If your charge is not satisfactorily settled and you want to protect your rights, you must also file a written charge with the EEOC. You must file with the EEOC within 300 days after the alleged wrongful act occurred, but you may file with the EEOC earlier, such as the same time you filed with your state agency. The EEOC will usually not take any action on your charge until the state agency decides what it will do. If the state agency does not satisfactorily settle your charge, you may ask the EEOC to go ahead with your claim. The procedure then is similar to the procedure in a state without an antidiscrimination law, as outlined above. You may look in the telephone directory of your state's largest city or its capital city for the address and phone number of your state agency. Most state agencies administering an antidiscrimination law are called a civil rights commission or a human rights commission. Your employer probably has posted on a bulletin board a poster printed for the EEOC or your state agency; the poster will tell where to write or phone for information.

If the EEOC is unable to settle satisfactorily (by "conciliation") a charge it believes has merit, the EEOC may file suit for you in a federal district court.

Many cities have an ordinance prohibiting discrimination. The EEOC may require that you file a charge with your city's agency and

Other remedies

give the city agency sufficient time to investigate and to conciliate your charge. Other remedies for discrimination include your hiring a private attorney to sue for violation of your civil rights under certain federal laws passed in 1866 and 1871. Some courts have also held that the U.S. Constitution protects some of your rights to be free of discrimination in seeking or maintaining employment.

Your proof   If you file a charge, claiming, for example, racial discrimination, you may be required to show that you belong to a racial minority, that you applied for and were qualified for a job for which that employer was seeking applicants, that you were rejected for the job, and that after your rejection the job remained open and the employer continued to seek applicants from persons having qualifications similar to yours. Keep a record of names and dates when particular incidents occurred. If you can show facts similar to these, the employer is considered to have violated the law unless he can show some non-discriminatory reason for rejecting you. You may then attempt to show that the reason the employer gave for not hiring you was a "pretext" for discrimination.

Pre-employment inquiries   Employers are not permitted to make certain inquiries before hiring an individual. For example, most of the antidiscrimination laws are interpreted to prohibit questioning an applicant whether he or she is married, or has children, unless the requirements of the job are such that it can be done only by males or females. An employer may ask if there is any reason why

the employer's usual work attendance requirements cannot be met. An employer cannot ask a
female applicant if she is pregnant but she may
be asked if she knows of any reason why she
cannot work regularly each day for the next
year. Photographs cannot be required of all
applicants, unless there is a specific job requirement, such as a model, which would justify this
requirement. Jobs may not be normally classified or advertised as "male" or "female" jobs.

Federal and state laws prohibit discrimination
against an applicant or employee based upon
"national origin," which is often interpreted to
mean the country of the person's ancestors, not
race or color. If an employer requires a minimum height and weight of an applicant for a
particular job, the employer may be required to
show that size is a "bona fide occupational requirement" of the job, that only individuals who
meet that height and weight or size requirement
could satisfactorily perform the job. Minimum
height or weight requirements may result in
discrimination against Mexican-Americans or females. Courts have ruled, however, that U.S.
citizenship may be required for some jobs, such
as those involving national security or national
defense. An employer may require an applicant
to show a Social Security card and to ask if the
applicant can provide proof of U.S. citizenship
or an alien registration number if hired.

Inquiries made by an employer on an application for employment form or in interviews
concerning whether an applicant has been ar-
rested for violation of a law may be considered

to discriminate on the basis of race or color. Inquiries about convictions of a crime more than seven or so years ago may also be considered to be discrimination for race or color. However, if the job requires a bond, for example, due to handling cash or for employees in security or law enforcement, this question may be proper. Some states prohibit inquiring as to the type of military discharge a veteran has, on the theory that a less than honorable discharge is awarded more frequently to members of minority groups.

An inquiry as to a job applicant's religion is usually prohibited, but an employer may ask if there is any reason why the applicant would not be able to work weekends if necessary to perform the job. A few states prohibit discrimination against individuals with physical or mental handicaps. These laws have been interpreted to prohibit discrimination against fat people, homosexuals, alcoholics, disfigurement, and stupidity, unless the employer can show that the applicant cannot do the job. An employer may ask an applicant if he or she has any handicaps that would prevent the satisfactory performance of the particular job, but he may not be permitted to inquire as to any handicaps that may not be related to the fitness to do the particular job.

Affirmative action plans

Many employers, particularly those with government contracts, have established "affirmative action plans" in which they agree to give preference to applicants for employment of a particular race, color, sex, etc. Employers who sell to or perform services for the federal government also cannot discriminate against physically or mentally handicapped persons.

Sometimes these plans are found to have a quota required for members of each race or minority group and may be unlawful. However, courts have upheld the establishment of a quota system to eliminate the effects of past discrimination by giving preference to members of minority groups. Many employers, such as those in the construction industry, have signed a "home town plan" for a particular city and the surrounding area in which the employers and labor unions that "sign up" agree to give preference to members of minority groups when hiring apprentices or in training and promotions.

An employer is required by the federal Equal Pay Act and by similar laws in several states to pay the same rate for males or females for jobs that require substantially equal "skill, effort, and responsibility" and have similar working conditions. Rates paid to males cannot be reduced to make the rate equal for both sexes. Contact the U.S. Department of Labor, Wage-Hour Division, which is located in larger cities and in Washington, D.C., for more information.

Equal pay

The federal Age Discrimination Act prohibits the refusal to hire an applicant because of age, usually protecting only individuals age 40 or more, but under age 65. It is administered by the U.S. Department of Labor, Wage-Hour Division. More than half of the states also have laws prohibiting discrimination on the basis of age. These laws may be enforced by a state agency. If the employer's pension plan does not cover

Age

employees who are over a particular age, the employer may still be required to hire an individual between age 40 and 65 even though the individual would not be eligible for that pension plan. Advertisements for a "young man" or a "junior executive" may violate age discrimination laws.

Lie detectors

Some states make unlawful a requirement that a job applicant or employee take a lie detector (polygraph) test, although it may be permitted if the individual voluntarily agrees. A lie detector test may also be permitted for certain jobs such as law enforcement or the handling of cash or other security jobs. Some insurance or bonding companies require that applicants for jobs that require a bond must pass a lie detector test.

Other tests

If an employer uses a psychological or performance test for applicants and that test has an adverse impact on women or on minority group members, the employer may be required to show, if a charge of discrimination is filed, that the test has been properly "validated"— that it is a good measurement of the requirements of the job.

If individuals who do well on the test are shown to do the particular job well and applicants who do poorly on the test are shown to do poorly on the job, then the test may be validated and may be used to test applicants for the job. There are other ways to validate a test, which are more complicated.

If you are hired

If you are hired, you will be asked to show your social security number and to complete an

Internal Revenue Service W-4 form, listing the number of dependents for income tax withholding purposes. If the employer has written work rules, you should ask for a copy of those rules, or at your earliest opportunity borrow a copy and read those rules. If the employer has an employee handbook, or a written outline of benefits for its employees, you should also get a copy of that handbook or outline. You should inquire as to the rate of pay per hour, week, or other time period that you will be receiving, and the hours that you will be expected to work. You should also learn exactly when you are to report to work and who is your immediate boss. You should then ask your boss exactly what you are expected to do.

part two

Your rights as an employee (whether or not there is a union)

Safety laws

The federal Job Safety and Health Act provides that each employee has a right to a place of employment that is free from recognized hazards that are causing or are likely to cause death or serious physical harm. The U.S. Department of Labor has established standards under the law for job safety and occupational health for various industries. If you believe that there is an unsafe condition that threatens serious harm or imminent danger to employees or others, you may make a complaint to the U.S. Department of Labor, Occupational Safety and Health Agency (OSHA). The OSHA will send an agent to make a physical inspection of the work area. An employee has the right to join the OSHA agent in his inspection of the hazard, but the employer may not be required to pay him for this time.

If the OSHA agent finds a violation of a safety or health standard, the agent issues a citation, either then or later by certified mail, listing the hazard. The proposed penalty is also stated. The citation or notice must be "promptly posted" on the bulletin board by the employer. An employer has only 15 working days to appeal a citation or a proposed penalty. If the hazard is not corrected, the OSHA may schedule a hearing before a hearing officer and he will later issue a report determining whether a penalty should be imposed upon the employer.

Each employee has a duty to comply with the safety and health standards and all rules, regulations, and orders issued under the law. Employees have a duty to familiarize themselves with and use safety devices made available to them by the employer, such as safety goggles, face shields, and gloves.

OSHA requires that a poster be posted for employees to read notifying them of the address of the OSHA agent. Employers are required to maintain accurate records and to make periodic reports of deaths, injuries and illnesses, other than minor injuries requiring only first aid treatment. Employers are also required to maintain accurate records of exposure by each employee to toxic materials or harmful physical agents considered in the law to be harmful. Each employee has access to the records showing the amount of his exposure to these toxic or harmful materials.

About half of the states have job safety and occupational health laws that have been approved by the U.S. Department of Labor. In these states, alleged violations of the state safety law should be reported to the state agency that administers the law. This is a separate agency in some states, but in most states it is under the Department of Labor or Industry.

The National Labor Relations Act permits an employee or employees to refuse to work because of "abnormally dangerous conditions for work at the place of employment." This is not considered to be a "strike." However, the employees may be required to show by "ascertainable, objective evidence" that an abnormally dangerous condition exists, not merely that they believe the conditions are abnormally dangerous.

Wage and hour laws

The federal Wage and Hour law, in general, requires a minimum rate of $2.10 per hour until January 1, 1976, when the minimum became $2.30 per hour. For employees covered by the laws only since 1966 (mostly those working for an "enterprise" with gross sales of less than one million dollars per year, or hospitals, schools, or local government), the minimum rate is 10 cents less until January 1, 1977, when the minimum will be $2.30. Agricultural employees must be paid $1.80 in 1975, $2.00 in 1976, $2.20 in 1977, and $2.30 in 1978.

Minimum wages

Employees must be paid time and one-half or more for hours worked over 40 per week. In a hospital, a work period of 80 hours in 14 calendar days is permitted and employees must be

Overtime

paid time and one-half over 80 hours worked in
this period or over 8 hours worked per day.
Federal law does not usually require payment
of overtime for over 8 hours worked in a day,
except for companies selling supplies to or who
are working on construction projects for the federal government. The law does not require that
an employer consider time paid for but not
worked (such as paid holidays, sick leave, or
vacations) as time worked, to determine if an
employee is entitled to time and one-half pay.
Federal law does not require extra pay for holiday work as such—extra pay is required only if
it is time actually worked over 40 hours per
week. Many union contracts and practices of
employers, however, provide for extra or "premium" pay for worked holidays.

Maids and housekeepers   Domestic service employees such as maids or
housekeepers in a private home must be paid
at least the minimum wage stated above if they
are paid at least $50 in a "calendar quarter"
by the employer, or if they are employed in
domestic service at least eight hours per week,
in total, for one or more employers. However,
companions for aged or infirmed persons or
casual babysitters are not covered by the minimum wage law.

Students   There are many exemptions to the overtime
and minimum wage law. Full time students must
be paid at least 85 percent of the applicable
minimum wage. An employer may hire up to
four such students without getting approval of
the Wage and Hour Division.

White collar exemptions   "White collar" administrative, professional,
or executive employees or outside sales persons

are not covered by the Wage and Hour Law requirements for overtime pay if they are regularly required to use independent judgment
and discretion. Executive or administrative employees must be paid at least $155.00 per week
and professional employees at least $170.00 per
week, to be "exempt" from the overtime pay
requirements. School administrative employees
and school teachers are also excluded from the
overtime requirements.

Police and fire

Police and fire department employees must
be paid an overtime rate for hours worked in
excess of a "work period," which may be only
a week, or may be as much as 28 days. They
may work an average of 60 hours per week in
1975 without the payment of overtime, or 58
hours in 1976, or 54 hours per week in 1977.

Procedure

If an individual believes that he has not received the minimum wage or overtime pay requirements of the federal Wage and Hour Law,
he may contact the U.S. Department of Labor,
Wage-Hour Division, nearest him and request
that they make an investigation. If they believe
that he is entitled to such payment, they will, if
necessary, go to court without charge to the individual to obtain the actual wages to which he
is entitled. If an individual prefers, he may hire
a private attorney and receive double the payment to which he is entitled. Do not wait too
long, however, since there is a cut-off date of
two years for most back pay claims.

Most of the laws requiring overtime pay also
require that accurate records be kept as to the
hours worked. Sometimes an employee completes his time card daily or weekly, listing the

starting and ending hours. Other employers require a time clock for more accurate records. If an employee alleges that he has not been paid for all hours worked, he should have accurate records as to the time actually worked. Of course, the employer should have accurate records if he believes that the employee was properly paid.

Working hours A new employee should ask his employer exactly when he is expected to begin work, and when he may leave work at the end of his work day. If work hours are not clear, problems sometimes arise whether an employee was "working" and is entitled to be paid. Working time includes all time spent during the workweek in physical or mental exertion (whether or not it is "burdensome" to the employee) controlled or required by the employer and pursued "necessarily and primarily for the benefit of the employer and his business."

If the employer requires or expects an employee to stay around his place of business, it is probably "working time." Even if an employee punches a time clock, the hours shown are not necessarily working time. For example, if he punches in early, when not required to, and performs no work, it is not working time. If an employee changes clothes before or after a shift it may not be work time unless it has customarily been treated as work time or a union contract requires that it be considered as work time. However, if the nature of the job, such as handling chemicals, requires showering and changing clothes, this may be work time. If an employee is waiting for work but is required to stay around the shop or office, it is usually work time if the time waiting is usually short and is unpredictable in length. If the employee is permitted to go home and to leave word where he may be called, it is probably not work time. Lunch time may be work time if an employee is required to stand by the employer's plant or office and to take calls or do other work as required. Time spent travelling from an employee's home to work and from the parking lot or within the plant to the place where he actually works is usually not considered to be work time. The above are only general rules; they may be changed by "past practice" of the employer or by a union contract.

Federal law requires that workers on most construction projects be paid at least the wages and "fringe benefits," prevailing in the area. Frequently the rate paid most often or is prevailing is the "union rate." A contractor may pay the prevailing wage rate and fringe benefits, or he may pay an amount equal to the fringe benefits in the form of additional wages. Other federal laws require the payment of prevailing wages by suppliers of equipment or supplies to, or for services done for, the federal government.

Prevailing wage laws

State wage and hour laws

Many states have a law similar to the federal law requiring payment of time and one-half after 40 hours worked per week. Some state laws also require time and one-half after eight

Minimum wages and overtime

hours worked per day. Most states have a minimum wage law, but the minimum required in many states is considerably below that required under federal law. Remember that some employers, particularly smaller employers, are not covered under the federal law.

Many state laws, like the federal Wage and Hour Law, control work in the home ("homework") by requiring that records be kept of the hours actually worked and that a minimum wage rate be paid.

Child labor
Most states have a law requiring that children under a stated age, such as 15 or 16, attend school when it is in session. State laws usually prohibit employment of children during periods when school is in session. A work permit, obtained either through the school principal or from the state department of labor, is required for children to work when school is in session, but outside of school hours. Children are prohibited at any time from doing many types of work considered to be hazardous, such as operating moving machinery, or harmful to their welfare and morals, such as work in a tavern.

Day of rest laws
Many states have a law prohibiting employees from working more than a stated number of days per week, or they require a "Sunday day of rest." Often these laws are written so that they apply only to women and children. However, the federal and state laws prohibiting discrimination on the basis of sex are often interpreted to make the "women and children's protective laws" unlawful, therefore many have been re-

pealed or they have been held to be invalid. Sometimes a law regulating the maximum hours or working conditions for women are interpreted to apply also to men.

If you have questions about whether your state has such a protective law, you may contact your state department of labor or the office of your state attorney general, usually located in the state capitol city.

Can an employee be required to work over-time? The answer to this question is compli-cated, but in general an employer can require an employee to work reasonable amounts of overtime as needed and he may be disciplined for failure to do so. If there is a union contract it may provide that an employee will be re-quired to work overtime only if he is given a stated number of hours' notice of the need for the overtime. Some employers post notices on bulletin boards outlining their overtime work requirements and the type of notice of scheduled overtime they will provide. If an employee is in a department that requires close teamwork, his absence or failure to work overtime may greatly hinder the entire department. If an employee has previous commitments, such as family plans or tickets for a show or game, he should tell his foreman as early as he can if he believes that overtime may be required.

Can overtime be required?

Emergency overtime may be required for em-ployers in a maintenance or repair job if equip-ment needs immediate repair. The nature of some types of jobs requires unscheduled over-time, such as hospital, fire, or police work.

Maximum hours   Many states have a law prohibiting women and children from working more than a stated number of hours daily or weekly. In other states a regulation or order, which usually has the same effect as a law passed by the legislature, limits the hours of work for women and children in various industries and jobs. Some of these laws have exceptions. Longer hours are permitted, for example, in seasonal industries handling perishable commodities. Many of these laws have been held by courts or fair employment practice agencies to be invalid where they are applied to women and not to men.

Other wage laws

Pay day   The laws of nearly all states provide that employees must have a regular pay day, usually at least every two weeks or twice a month. Most of the states require that employees be paid in "lawful money," which usually permits payment by check. A few states require that an employer provide a check cashing service, but employees may be charged a small fee for the cashing of the check.

Hold over of wages   In most states an employer is permitted to "hold over" wages for a period of time. For example, if an employee's work week ends Friday night the law permits an employer to hold over his wages, usually from 5 days to 30 days, before paying wages for that period of time. This hold-over period is permitted for computing the amount that employees earn, the deductions from their pay, and preparing their pay checks.

The laws of some states require that an employer give employees an itemized statement showing deductions, such as for income tax withholding, social security, union dues, hospital insurance, or similar items. Some states require that any deductions other than those required by federal or state law be authorized by the employee in writing before the employer can deduct it from his pay check.

Employees are entitled in nearly all states to prompt payment of wages due if they are discharged. Some states also provide that employees who quit are entitled to prompt payment of all wages due. Many states permit the employer to delay the payment of the check until the next regular pay day.

If an employee is issued tools, uniforms, special clothing, or other equipment by his employer, and he has a loss of such equipment due to theft or other reasons, or if such equipment is damaged or destroyed due to other than normal wear and tear, the employer may be permitted to deduct this from the employees pay. Some states require that the employee authorize in writing any deduction before it is legally enforceable. If any employee was not provided with a locker or other storage area which can be locked, and if he was not careless in failing to put away his tools, some employers do not require that he pay for the loss.

Federal and various state safety laws require

Statement of deductions

Pay on leaving

Tools and special clothing

that protective clothing or equipment such as hard hats, safety goggles, and safety-toe shoes be provided as needed to adequately safe-guard workers. A few state laws require that the employer pay for the equipment.

Money shortages

If an employee is responsible for handling money, such as a cashier or bank teller, and he has a shortage, he may be required to make up the difference by the deduction from his pay unless the employee can prove that it is not his fault. Some states do not permit an employer to make a deduction from an employee's pay for a cash shortage unless that employee is the only person with a key to that cash register.

If an employee is charged with a cash shortage can the employer require that he take a lie detector test? The laws vary from state to state on this. A few states prohibit an employer from requiring that an employee take a lie detector test and "pass it" in order to keep his job if he is charged with a cash shortage. An employee may, of course, voluntarily take a lie detector test, but he should have a clear written agreement beforehand that if he "passes" the test he will not be held liable for the cash shortage.

Garnishment of wages

Federal law limits the amount of an employee's earnings in any workweek that may be "garnished" by a creditor. Not more than 25 percent of "disposable" earnings in any week may be garnished, but an employee is entitled to keep 30 times the federal minimum wage that applies to him. Federal law prohibits an employer from discharging an employee for a first garnishment, but he may be discharged for a second garnishment. Contact the U.S. Department of Labor, Wage-Hour Division office nearest you for information. Some states have a similar law; contact your state Department of Labor for violations.

As pointed out above, a failure to hire or a discharge for a first garnishment may also violate federal or state "fair employment practices" laws, on the theory that blacks or members of minority races have their wages garnished more often than whites.

The United States Supreme Court has held that state laws must provide that creditors give an employee notice and an opportunity to be heard, before his wages can be garnished. The constitution's "due process" clause protects this right.

If an employer does not pay an employee the amount of wages due by agreement for the time he worked, some states permit an employee to make a written statement as to the amount due to the state labor department, which will then make an investigation and, if necessary, hold a hearing or authorize the state attorney general's office to go into court to collect the back wages. An employee may be asked to sign an assignment of his wage claim. If those back wages are for overtime worked over 40 hours per week or if the failure to receive those wages would result in payment to an employee of less than the minimum wage, then the Wage-Hour Division of the U.S. Department of Labor may help an employee collect those back wages. Many states will not help an employee collect back wage

Wage collections

claims other than for violations of the minimum wage law or an overtime payment law unless the amount is below a stated figure, such as $500. This varies from state to state. If the amount of a back wage claim exceeds this, an employee may have to hire a private attorney to help him collect the back wages, or if he is represented by a union, the union may help him collect the back wages.

If an employee is owed back wages and his employer is having financial problems with creditors, wage claims are given preferential treatment over most creditors' claims in all states. The federal bankruptcy law also gives employees' wage claims preference over many other creditors.

Meals, rest periods, and facilities

The laws of many states provide that an employee is entitled to a period free from work for a meal after a stated number of hours employment, usually five. Half an hour is the usual time provided. Many state laws require a paid rest period of 10 or 15 minutes near the middle of each half shift of 4 hours or more.

State laws frequently require a rest area, usually with a cot for female employees. Some laws require a toilet for each stated number of employees, and may require that separate restrooms be provided for males and females if there are more than a stated number of employees.

Most of the state laws requiring lunch and rest periods and restroom facilities apply only to female employees, but have been interpreted by courts or fair employment practice agencies to be invalid when limited to female employees.

Some decisions require that these laws be applied to male employees as well as to females, on the theory that if laws are applied only to one sex that it is discrimination against the other sex.

Many state laws prohibit the lifting of weights over a stated number of pounds by female employees. These laws are also sometimes interpreted to be in conflict with the laws prohibiting discrimination on the basis of sex. If an employer requires that someone be able to regularly lift weights of, for example, 35 pounds or more before being qualified for a particular job, the employer may be required to show that the job actually requires this ability. The employer cannot legally refuse to promote someone to that job solely because she is a female or because a state law prohibits females from lifting these weights. If the individual can show that she is physically capable of lifting such weights, she must be given the same consideration for the job as is given to male applicants. Many state safety laws provide that if a job requires lifting of heavy weights that the employees be instructed in the proper procedure to be used in lifting such weights. For jobs which require heavy lifting, employees should ask their boss or the employer's safety supervisor to show them the correct way to lift—it may prevent strains and years of pain in the back.

Weight lifting limitations

How to present a complaint to your employer

If you have a gripe, grievance, or complaint at work you may discuss it with your supervisor even though you do not have a union contract or even a union. Some "non-union" employers have a written grievance procedure even though there is no union representing the employees. To learn whether your employer has a written procedure, check your employee handbook or the bulletin board where notices for employees are posted, or ask your supervisor.

The first step in discussing a gripe or dispute is to decide exactly what your complaint is. Then discuss it with your immediate supervisor. If it is something that does not directly involve his area, the better rule is to at least let him know of the problem before discussing it with anyone outside the department. For example, if you believe that you were not paid for all of the hours you worked or that the rate of pay is wrong you should mention it to your supervisor. You may jointly agree that you or your supervisor should discuss it with someone from the payroll department, and then do so. Keep your supervisor informed. Remember that he has considerable control over your future with that employer. Before going "over his head" to his supervisor or the personnel department about a complaint, you may ask the advice of an older employee whose judgment is respected on whether to take your complaint elsewhere.

Before discussing a gripe or grievance, try to be sure of the "facts." None of us is always correct. It can be embarrassing if we go to the supervisor with a complaint that he did something wrong, threaten to go higher up, and then to learn that it was our mistake and not the employer's mistake. At an early step in a grievance discussion, you and your supervisor should attempt to decide what happened and avoid taking a firm position or getting mad. You should explain your position without arguing or losing patience. For example, if the dispute is one over pay, you should take your pay check stub and your time card or similar record with you when you discuss it, and make an opening statement such as, "It seems to me that there is an error for my pay last week. I don't believe I was paid for the extra time I worked last Tuesday. It's on my time card but not on my paycheck stub."

If your complaint is not settled to your satisfaction, you should consider going the next step up, such as to your supervisor's boss. It is better to go "through channels" since it keeps everyone informed. Some employers provide that you may contact the personnel department if you have a complaint that is not settled at the level of your immediate supervisor. Some personnel departments welcome such discussion and attempt to help you in resolving complaints. In other companies you are expected to strictly follow the "channels." Find out how it is done in your company before taking action.

If you have a dispute over some matter, such as pay or working overtime, it is better to bring it up for discussion as soon as possible. Do not wait several weeks before bringing it up, since the records showing what happened may be difficult to find and the people involved may forget what happened. However, if you are quite angry at the time you discover what you believe to be improper treatment, you should probably "sleep on it" and not discuss it with your boss when you are still mad. You may say things you will regret later, and your boss may also get mad. After you have "cooled off" a little you are more likely to try to decide exactly what happened and to work with your boss rather than against him in settling the complaint.

If your complaint is complicated it will help if at the end of your shift you go home and write down in detail exactly what has happened. If you have a continuing problem at work, it will be helpful if each time such an incident occurs that you jot down on a piece of scratch paper:

When did the incidents occur—date and time?
What happened?
Where?
Who saw or heard it?

You may then put your scratch notes together to write in detail exactly what happened.

If your employer has a rule against leaving your work area without permission, you should follow that rule before leaving to discuss a grievance. Even though your complaint is valid, if you leave your work area to discuss it with your boss or the personnel department you could be disciplined for *another* reason—leaving your work area without permission.

The National Labor Relations Board and some state agencies protect the right of *employees* (usually two or more) to complain about some matter at work or a working condition. This is called "concerted activity." However, if you complain only about something personal to you, this is not concerted activity for which the NLRB will protect you. Even if there is no union that represents employees, if a group of two or more employees complain to the boss about some working condition, it will probably be found to be concerted activity. Your right to engage in that concerted activity will be protected by the NLRB from disciplinary action unless you do something clearly wrong, such as fighting with your boss. If a union represents you, be sure to notify it of your complaint if it it not settled by you and your boss. See the discussion in Part Three (If a union is recognized: Grievances) for a summary of what to do.

Antidiscrimination laws

Federal law and laws in over half of the states prohibit discrimination in employment because of race, color, national origin, religion, or sex. Federal law and most states prohibit discrimination on the basis of age; these laws usually protect only individuals ages 40 through 64. More than 200 cities also have ordinances that prohibit discrimination in employment. For additional discussion of these laws and the procedure used in enforcing them, see pages 6 through 14 above.

The type of activities protected by most of the laws include hiring, wages, hours, working conditions, promotion, lay-off, discharge, and re-call. Most of the laws prohibiting discrimination apply not only to employers but also to labor unions and private or state-federal employment agencies.

In some states if a group of employees refuse to cooperate with an employer in his policy of permitting employees of a particular race, color, national origin, religion, sex, or age to have equal rights, the employer may file an unfair practice charge against his employees or a union that represents them.

Prohibited practices

Typical employment practices that have been found to violate fair employment practice laws are listed below:

To segregate or classify employees by race, color, national origin, religion, sex, or age.

To have separate seniority lists based upon race, color, national origin, religion, sex, or age.

To classify jobs as male or female jobs or white or black jobs, or Mexican-American or "Anglo" jobs.

To permit only males, not females, to work an evening or night shift or to work overtime.

To refuse to consider females for jobs that require heavy lifting or the operation of equipment.

To refuse to consider females for apprentice trainees or other jobs that require a long period of training.

To pay males a higher wage rate than females performing equal or similar work, performed under simliar working conditions.

To require that all job applicants or individuals for promotion have a high school education where there is no showing that this requirement is sufficiently related to the demands of the job. (An employer may be required to consider the passing of an approved General Education Development test as the equivalent of a high school education.)

Refusal to promote individuals or to discharge employees for having a poor credit rating or for receiving a first garnishment of their wages.

An employer or a union must make a "reasonable accommodation" to an employee's religious beliefs. However, the NLRB and the courts have ruled that an employee may be properly discharged if he refuses to pay any dues or fees to a union that has a contract with a "union shop clause" with the employer. If an employee has religious objections to joining a union, he is probably not required to join, but he may be required to pay union dues and initiation fees. If an employee objects for religious reasons to even paying money to a union, he should offer to pay regularly an equal amount to a charitable organization. The union may insist upon the right to name that organization. **Religion**

An employer may be permitted to prefer individuals of a particular race, color, national origin, citizenship, religion, sex or age if the employer can show that it has a business purpose in giving preference and that purpose is so essential to the safe and efficient operation of the business as to override any discriminatory impact against a particular group. **Business necessity**

If an employer makes promotions on the basis of the supervisor's "subjective" evaluation of employees "ability, merit, and capacity" and the supervisors are not given instructions as to safeguards to avoid discriminatory practices, then the employer may be found to favor or to discriminate against particular groups based upon race, color, or other classifications.

If an employer prohibits long hair or long moustaches by male employees, but does not prohibit females from having long hair, it may be discrimination on the basis of sex. However, the trend in court decisions is to permit the employer to require a high standard of grooming, particularly where it can show a business necessity. For example, one court stated that long hair has nothing to do with sex, since either males or females may have long or short hair. If an employer has a business purpose in doing so, such as in a restaurant or food processing plant, or where long hair is a safety hazard, it may clearly require males or females to have short hair or to wear a hair net.

If promotions or demotions are based partly upon seniority, as they are with most employers, and the use of seniority results in promotions for a lesser proportion of members of a minority group, such as women or blacks, than it does for white males, the seniority system may be found "to retain the effects of past discrimination"; therefore, it may be unlawful. In the filling of jobs, some employers have switched to the use of company-wide or department-wide seniority to enable women or minority groups, who had been limited to only one department, to get a better chance at the jobs in all departments.

If an employer has had a past practice of giving preference in particular jobs to males or to females, it may be required to advertize to both sexes that it has vacant positions and that employees of either sex may apply. This may be in the form of:

1. Asking women and minority groups to prepare a list for the supervisor or personnel department of jobs for which they want to be considered, or
2. An announcement posted on bulletin boards of each job vacancy, or
3. A formal job bidding procedure. (Job bidding usually requires written job descriptions or job qualifications which are made available to employees, the posting on bulletin boards for a stated number of days of a notice of a job vacancy, and the sending in of a written request or "bid" by each employee interested in that job.)

Several states prohibit discrimination against handicapped workers and require that an employer make "reasonable" changes in its practices to enable the handicapped to fill jobs they would otherwise be unable to fill. A similar federal law applies to employers who sell supplies to or perform services for the federal government. Changes frequently required are improvements of access of the handicapped to the plant and its facilities (such as ramps rather than stairways and the use of wider aisles), the restructuring of jobs, and the changing of equipment. The federal law is administered by the U.S. Department of Labor Employment Standards Administration. State laws are usually administered by the state's civil rights commission or similar agency. If an individual is physically or mentally handicapped but can do a particular job he must be given fair consideration if he applies and there is a vacant position.

How to discuss your job performance with your boss

Most medium size and larger employers have a formal system set up to rate the performance or merit of each employee on a regular basis, such as once a year. In some companies the supervisor completes a performance analysis sheet without discussing it with the employee or making it available to him. The trend however, is to make copies of the performance rating available to employees and to discuss it with them.

The goal of most performance rating or analysis is to see how an employee is doing in comparison with the fictitious average employee. Some employers also rate an employee's present performance or compare it with his performance at an earlier period to see whether he has improved. A rating can be important for the employee's future. Many employers use the performance analysis sheets as a guide in determining whether an individual is eligible for promotion to a higher paying job, whether he will get a merit increase in pay, and, if there is a layoff, whether he should be laid off or retained.

A major reason for having performance analysis is to let the employee know what the supervisor believes to be his weak points or failings so that both can set up a program to improve those points. Obviously, if the employer has a practice of not discussing employee performance ratings with the employee, they do not get this benefit.

Some performance ratings are only one page long with various items to check, such as quantity of work, quality, accuracy, neatness of work, knowledge of work, adaptibility to change in work methods, personality, cooperation, planning work, and leadership. Some of the forms have a simple scale such as superior, above average, average, below average, or inferior. One problem with this kind of rating system is that many supervisors, busy with other problems they think are more pressing, take the easy way out, by rating almost all employees as "average" or "above average."

An employee should determine whether his employer has a formal written job performance procedure and if an employee's performance is discussed with him by the supervisor. If there is such a procedure, then an employee can use it to help further his career. An employee should convince his boss that he is really interested in doing a better job. In the interview, do not get mad and flare-up when he points out that you are weak in a particular area. The employee should inquire as to why the supervisor believes that he is weak in that area and indicate that he will try to improve. Even if the supervisor has not been satisfied with the employee's work in the past, his attitude will help to convince the supervisor that he is trying to improve.

It will be more effective if an employee looks at his performance analysis as if the rating is for some stranger, a third person, and not himself. Treat it as if job performance and not the individual is being rated. An employee can probably change and improve his job performance, but it would be much more difficult to change his total personality.

Work rules

The "common law of the shop"

You have probably heard of the "common law" of England and the United States. This has been developed over many years by custom and by court decisions, rather than by statutes passed by legislatures. There is also the "common law of the shop," dealing with the relations among employees, employers, and unions. This common law has developed by custom, decisions of arbitrators, by boards such as the NLRB, and by court decisions.

One source of information about the "common law of the shop" is to examine the published decisions of arbitrators in labor cases, such as those published by the Bureau of National Affairs or the American Arbitration Association. Many large city libraries or law libraries maintain a set of these decisions. The decisions are often classified by subject or the issue involved in the dispute, such as discharge or discipline, promotions, transfers, layoffs, severance pay, seniority, employee benefits, wages, overtime and premium pay, picketing and strikes, jurisdictional disputes, and management rights.

The total of customs, practices, and rules applying to employees of a particular employer might be called the "common law" of the employer. It tends to be fairly uniform in a particular industry. Any employee who has worked in industry learns "how things are done" where he is employed. Often many of the customs are not expressly stated in a union contract, contract interpretation manual, company policy manual for employees, or by printed rules passed out to employees or posted on a bulletin board. If a union agent is attempting to organize employees or to negotiate a first contract with an employer he usually has many meetings with employees to learn how things are done where they are employed.

Many employers have written rules and employment practices, either in the form of a handbook distributed to each employee, or work rules given to employees or posted on a bulletin board. Some employers have both. These work rules are often in considerable detail and are similar to a typical union collective bargaining agreement. If your employer has written work rules or an employee handbook, you should get a copy and read them. If there is a union contract and some provision in it clearly conflicts with a work rule or employee handbook, the union contract is probably controlling. However, it is common for company work rules to "supplement" a union contract.

Rights of veterans

If an individual left a job (not a temporary job) to volunteer for military service for the United States, or if he was drafted, he probably has rights to his old job or a similar job. He must reapply with the employer within 90 days after his discharge. If he was hospitalized after military service he may apply when released from the hospital; he may keep his job rights for up to a year in a hospital.

An individual on military leave is entitled to all benefits employees on a leave of absence earn. If benefits, such as vacations, are earned for that employer only for employees while working, and not for those on leave of absence, then employees are probably not entitled to vacation benefits for time spent in the military service. If employees receive "automatic" or "general" wage increases based upon length of time with the employer, without a required training period, employees on military leave are probably entitled to those benefits. They are entitled to promotions if they are based only upon length of service with the employer and not ability. They may not be discharged without "cause" or a good reason for a year after returning.

The above is summary of federal law. If you have additional questions about military rights, contact the Veterans Administration or the U.S. Department of Labor office nearest you. Nearly all states also have laws protecting veterans employment rights. Contact a nearby state employment office for information.

For employees in the armed or active reserves many states require an employer to provide a leave of up to 15 days or so a year for active military duty. Employees may be required to take an unpaid leave or to use their vacation time. Some union contracts require that an employer pay the difference between an employee's regular pay and the pay received from the military, so that an employee is "made whole" for his military leave time.

Fringe benefits

Fringe benefits are any benefits an employee has as a result of his job other than direct wages or salaries. Fringe benefits include:

1. Pay for time not worked—paid vacations, paid holidays, paid sick leave, disability pay, rest periods, paid lunch periods, layoff or termination pay, layover time, standby pay, unworked call-in pay, reporting pay, set-up time, break-down time, cleanup and checkout time, jury duty pay, voting time pay, training and education, and time spent on grievances,

2. Benefit plans paid in part or entirely by the

employer, such as hospital insurance, group life insurance, dental insurance, prescription drug insurance, vision care insurance, legal services insurance, and pension or profit sharing plans,

3. Legally required payments, such as unemployment compensation, workman's compensation (industrial accident insurance), and the employer's half of Social Security.

4. Premium pay for time worked, such as overtime, Sunday, holiday, or weekend pay, shift premiums, job differentials, and call-in pay, and

5. Miscellaneous fringe costs, such as uniforms and special clothing, suggestion plan awards, safety awards, employee entertainment and recreation, cafeteria or food service costs, bonuses, discounts on goods and services (including corporate stocks) bought from the employer, child care for working mothers, taxi fare for employees working nights, low-interest loans from the employer, moving expenses, travel pay, board and lodging, free parking, and the use of a company car for personal affairs.

It is unlikely that any employer provides all of the fringe benefits listed above. Some industries traditionally have many "fringes"; other industries have few. Industries with low labor costs and high costs for "capital equipment" may be able to afford high wages and good fringe benefits. Other industries—those that use a lot of hand labor and are highly com-

petitive, may not be able to absorb wage increases of even a few cents an hour. Wage increases that can quickly be passed on to the
customer by some employers may force other
employers into the bankruptcy court.

If an employer is a good businessman he has
probably computed the cost of the fringe benefits
he pays to employees. This is a cost of doing
business the same as is an employee's wage or
salary. When an employee compares his income
with that of his friends, or if he is considering
changing jobs, he should not forget to consider
the fringe benefits. An employee doesn't have
to pay income tax on many fringe benefits. Yet
all of these fringes are to the employer a cost of
doing business. The legally required fringe
benefits (workman's compensation, unemployment compensation, and the employer's half of
Social Security payments) alone equals about
10 to 12 percent of direct wages.

Let's take a look at the cost to the employer of
pay for time not worked. This includes paid
vacation, paid holiday, and paid sick leave or
accident pay. If an employee gets two weeks of
paid vacation a year, plus eight paid holidays,
and he takes an average of four days paid sick
leave a year, then he is paid a total of 22 days
per year when he is not working. If he is paid
for 52 weeks work, five days a week, this is 260
days. If 22 of those days paid are not worked,
then his pay for time not worked costs the employer about $8\frac{1}{2}$ percent of the employee's
regular straight time pay.

If an individual is good at arithmetic he can

estimate how much all of the fringe benefits are worth.

Employee benefit plans

Hospital
insurance

Hospital or health care insurance is often provided by employers under a group insurance plan. Employees are not usually required to have a physical examination or to furnish other satisfactory evidence of good health prior to enrolling in group plans, if they enroll within a particular time period. Many plans permit employees to enroll without an exam within a stated number of days or months after they are first employed. Some plans do not permit part time or temporary employees to be covered by the plan. Many plans will not pay any benefits until a stated time period, such as 90 days of employment, has elapsed, but premium payments may be required even for this period.

In a "contributory" plan, the employee pays all or part of the monthly insurance premium. In a "non-contributory" plan the employer pays for the entire cost.

A typical hospital insurance plan pays a stated percentage, such as 80 percent, of the basic hospital costs such as for a bed in a two-bed or a four-bed ward, meals, required surgical expense, doctor's visits while a patient is in the hospital, required diagnostic X rays, and laboratory expenses.

Many plans have a stated maximum amount for "major medical" coverage, such as $20,000 or $50,000 for an employee and his dependents.

This may be the life-time maximum that particular plan will pay out on behalf of that employee or his dependents. Many plans have a stated deductible amount, such as $100. This means that the major medical coverage will pay for hospital and other covered expenses for hospital patients *only* after the employee pays the deductible amount. The major medical coverage usually pays a stated percentage, such as 80 percent of the "reasonable" costs above the deductible amount.

Some hospital plans do not cover maternity or obstetrical benefits, or there is no coverage until after a stated period of time, such as nine months after premiums have been paid on behalf of that employee.

Hospital insurance plans usually permit all of the employee's dependents to be covered at a stated additional amount per month for each dependent.

Most hospital insurance plans expressly state that they will not pay for any illness or injury for which the employee may be compensated by any other plan such as Medicare (available to individuals under the Social Security Act, see below), industrial accident, or if the individual recovers money damages as a result of injury in any other accident. You should know:

1. When to sign up for your hospital insurance; how to sign up;
2. When premium payments must begin, and who pays;
3. When you are eligible for coverage;

whether your dependents are eligible for coverage; and, if so, who makes the payment;

4. How and where to file a claim for the insurance; where to get a claim form; who fills it out, whether claims are paid only after you pay a deductible amount;

5. Whether there is a separate deductible amount for each of your dependents before the plan pays out the money; and

6. Whether you must first pay the hospital and doctor bills and apply to the insurance plan for a reimbursement.

Most plans pay the hospital or doctor's bill and the hospital or doctor will then bill you for the additional amount not covered by your plan.

If you are leaving your employer you should inquire as to whether you can continue the hospital insurance plan on an individual policy basis. You may avoid having to take a doctor's examination if you can convert your group plan to an individual plan, but you can expect the premium rates to be higher.

If you itemize income tax deductions, half of the payments made by you in excess of $150 each year, may be listed as a deduction on your income tax.

Some hospital insurance plans have additional coverage such as accidental death and dismemberment (loss of an arm, leg, eye, etc.) wherever this occurs, whether on the job or elsewhere. Some plans include an accident and sickness weekly income insurance; if you are unable to work because of an accident or sickness, you will receive a stated amount of weekly benefit (such as $50) up to a maximum of a stated number of weeks (such as 26 weeks). Most of these plans do not pay benefits if you receive compensation from workman's compensation or similar industrial accident insurance for injuries or accidents occurring at work.

Many hospital insurance plans have a fee schedule for surgery and anesthesia in which a stated amount is allowed for the doctor or other medical personnel for particular procedures such as types of surgery. If the costs for these operations or procedures are higher in your area the plan will not pay that additional amount. You will be charged for it.

If there is a hospital insurance plan available to you, you should get a copy of the booklet that explains the coverage in detail.

Many employers have available a group life insurance plan in which an employee is charged a stated amount per month for each thousand dollars of insurance. The amount an employee can sign up for is usually based upon his annual earnings. Some employers pay the entire amount of the premium costs, others pay a stated portion, while in other plans the employee pays the entire amount. One advantage of a group life insurance plan is that you will probably not be required to take a physical examination or to show other proof of good health before enrolling in the plan. You should determine whether your employer has such a plan, when you are eligible to sign up for it, how to sign up, how much you are eligible for, who pays for it, and

Group life insurance

how payments are made. Your employer will usually deduct your portion of the cost from your paycheck once a month.

Prescription drug insurance

Some employers have a prescription drug insurance plan, which provides that the plan will pay the "reasonable" cost of drugs prescribed in writing by physicians, dentists, and similar medical personnel. Some plans permit you to buy the drug any place, but the plan administrator or trustees may not pay more than a rate they consider to be reasonable for that drug in your area. Many of the plans only pay a stated percentage of the cost of the drug, such as 80 percent.

If you obtain a drug without a prescription most plans do not pay for it. As with all medical-type insurance plans, you may be required to file a written claim (turn in the receipt) within a stated number of days, and if you wait too long the plan may not pay anything.

Vision care

Some employers have a vision care plan that pays in full for an eye examination and for a stated number of lenses and frames per year. Some plans may pay for the cost of contact lens when a physician certifies that they are required, and not for cosmetic purposes. The plans often do not cover the replacing of broken lenses or frames.

Dental insurance

Some employers have a dental insurance program, whereby contributions are made monthly for dental care coverage for the employee, and sometimes his dependents, up to a certain age. The plans usually pay a low percentage, such as 60 percent, for the first year, then an increasing amount for 3 or 4 years upon the condition that each person covered visit his dentist regularly (each 6 months or each year) to have preventive work done, such as cleaning teeth and filling cavities. Many of the plans have a "schedule of allowances" for various services performed by dentists or similar medical personnel. Services which are done purely for cosmetic purposes are usually not covered. Dentures may be provided as necessary, with a stated number over a given period of time.

Some employers provide for a prepaid legal services program in which a stated contribution rate is paid to participating attorneys or law firms. The plans are either "open end," in which an individual covered by the legal services program may go to any attorney in the area, or "closed end," in which the plan pays only for legal fees for the particular attorneys or law firms who participate in the plan. Many of the legal services plans do not compensate or cover an employee who has a legal "cause of action" against either his employer or the union that represents the employee.

Prepaid legal services

The plans often provide a stated amount of consulting work and may include particular services such as a divorce action, custody of children, or the probate of a will.

If an employee is sick and cannot be at work he should call his employer not later than the beginning of the shift which he is expected to be at work. Many employers require that an employee provide a statement signed by a physician before he is eligible for sick leave. Some

Paid sick leave

employers will not pay sick leave for the first one or two day's absence from work. An employee should get a copy of any requirements for his plan or ask his supervisor or the personnel department what are the requirements for the plan.

Most paid sick leave is earned at a stated amount per month of regular employment, such as one-half day of paid sick leave for every month of employment. Many employers limit the amount of sick leave which may be accumulated, such as two weeks maximum.

Many employees prefer to use all of their sick leave if they are sick, rather than to take an unpaid leave of absence or to use paid vacation time accumulated while sick. Many employers permit an employee who has used up accumulated sick leave to take accrued vacation time so that the employee may not lose any pay.

If a member of an employee's family is sick and the employee is needed to stay home and take care of that person, most sick leave plans do not permit the use of sick leave. The usual rule is that sick leave can be used only for the employee and not for dependents of the employee. Some plans permit the use of paid sick leave for appointments with a physician, dentist, or other medical personnel. An employee may be required, however, to take a full day or a half day even for a short appointment. An employee should check with his supervisor or personnel department to see what his employer's rules are.

If an employee is injured at work he should immediately report it to his supervisor. The supervisor will probably be required to complete a form for the Occupational Safety and Health Act, for his state's safety department, or for the employer's insurance carrier, or for all three. If an employee is required to have a physician check him, some employers may require that the physician certify in writing if the employee is unable to return to work for that day. If for example, an employee is injured in the morning and is taken to a physician and is given minor treatment, many employers require that he return to work for the completion of his shift unless he obtains a written statement from the physician that he should not return to work that day.

Injuries and workman's compensation

If an employee is injured on the job, many plans permit him to use any accrued sick leave, and he may be entitled to use any accrued vacation time, as pointed out above.

If an employee is covered under Social Security, he may be eligible for disability benefits if he is expected to be disabled for 12 months or more, or if his present illness or injury will probably result in his death. An individual may check with the local federal Social Security office to determine whether he is eligible for disability payments. In general, if an individual is younger than age 24 he needs credit for one and one-half years of work for which his employer paid Social Security benefits in the last 3-year period. If he is age 24 through 30 he needs credit for half of the time he has worked since age 21, and if he is age 31 or older he may need credit for at least 5 years' work out of the last 10 years.

If an individual receives disability benefits under Social Security his dependents are probably also entitled to benefits. Everyone must check with the Social Security office before getting disability benefits. They are not paid automatically.

If an individual is injured on the job or if he suffers an occupational disease caused partially by his employment, he is probably entitled to benefits under his state's Workman's Compensation law. If he is injured or becomes ill he should see a doctor and request that he complete the forms to entitle him to Workman's Compensation. If he loses an arm, a leg, a toe, a finger, etc., he may be entitled to a lump sum payment. If an individual is "partially disabled," he may be entitled to a regular monthly payment, but less than normal benefits.

Workman's Compensation premiums in many states is paid entirely by the employer; in some states the employee also makes payments. In most states an employer may buy Workman's Compensation insurance from a private insurance company, or large employers may "self-insure," or an employer may pay for the Workman's Compensation insurance operated by the state government.

If an employee is disabled at work he may be entitled to payments both under his state's Workman's Compensation law and under federal Social Security. He will probably receive, however, only about 80 percent of his normal weekly or monthly wage from both plans combined. Most state Workman's Compensation plans pay benefits for total disability equal to about one-half to two-thirds of the state's average wage. Be sure to inquire about "vocational rehabilitation" training programs which may be available to give an individual free training for more suitable employment.

If an employee is covered by Workman's Compensation and is injured on the job he probably cannot successfully sue his employer for the injury. If an employee is hurt in connection with his job by a "third party" he can probably sue that third party, but he may not get Workman's Compensation benefits. See your state industrial accident commission or state department of labor or ask an attorney for more information.

Social Security

Most employees, except those in agriculture or those covered by the Railroad Retirement Act and some local government employees, are under the federal Social Security plan. The employer pays 5.85 percent of an employee's salary, up to a stated amount, currently $15,300 per year, into the plan. An equal amount is deducted from the employee's pay. If an employee earns more than $50 in a calendar quarter (for example, January, February, and March), his employer is required to deduct for Social Security and to make an equal payment himself. This gives the employee "one quarter of work credit." Self-employed individuals, such as business owners or farmers, receive four quarters of work credit for a year when they have self-employment net profit of four hundred dollars or more. An individual must have a minimum number of quarters of work credit before he is entitled to any benefits under Social Security payment when he reaches the required age. However, the amount of the check depends upon his average earnings over a period of years.

Every two or three years an individual should write to the Social Security administration to get a copy of a statement as to how much has been paid by employers on his behalf. If the information furnished shows that his account has not been credited for all of the payments, he should notify the local Social Security office promptly in writing because the statute of limitations is only slightly more than three years. If he delays, it may be too late.

Your local Social Security office can help you estimate the amount of your Social Security retirement check.

If you will be age 65 in six months you should apply for benefits at your local Social Security office. You are not paid benefits automatically upon reaching your 65th birthday—you must apply for the benefits. There is a time delay so that if you act early you will start receiving checks when you reach age 65. Male or female workers may get Social Security retirement payments at age 62, but the monthly amount is less than would be received if they wait until age 65 to retire. When you apply for benefits, take your Social Security number, proof of age such as a birth certificate or baptismal certificate, your marriage certificate if you're applying for wife's or widow's benefits, your children's birth certificates if you're applying for them, and a copy of the W-2 income tax return received last year from your employer.

If you continue to work at age 65 you may have earnings from employment of as much as $2,760 in a year without your benefits being reduced. If your earnings from employment exceed that amount you will have a reduction in the Social Security benefits, based upon the amount of your earnings. When you reach age 72 there is no reduction in your retirement benefits as a result of earnings.

Your husband or wife is entitled to benefits based upon your earnings, and any dependent children are also entitled to benefits. If you, the worker, die, your survivors may be entitled to benefits also. If your parents are dependent upon you, the Social Security retiree, for support then your parents may also be entitled to share in your Social Security benefits. Your survivors are entitled to a lump sum to cover burial expenses. You may be entitled to payments based upon earnings of your former husband even if you are divorced.

If you are age 65 or older or blind or disabled you may be eligible for regular monthly payments to supplement your income. If the "resources" or things you own, such as savings (but

Supplemental security income

probably not counting your home and household goods) are valued at less than $1,500 for a single person or $2,250 for a couple, and if your income is low, you may be eligible. To find out see your local Social Security Office.

Medical insurance

The federal Social Security also includes Medicare hospital insurance, and medical insurance (sometimes called "Medicaid"). If you are age 65 and are receiving Social Security retirement benefits you are eligible for either plan. If you are under age 65 and are entitled to Social Security disability benefits for a period of 24 or more consecutive months, you may also be entitled to Medicare insurance. If you, your wife, your husband, or children are insured under Social Security and need dialysis treatment or a kidney transplant, you may also be entitled to Medicare.

Medicare hospital insurance benefits give you up to 90 days care in a hospital. You must pay the first $92 in cost. After 60 days of hospital care, you must pay $23 a day. You also have a "lifetime reserve" of 60 additional days in a hospital; you must pay for the first $46 each day. If your medical condition requires a stay in a qualified health facility such as a nursing home after a hospital stay, you may be entitled to up to 100 days of care. Medicare insurance pays for all of the covered services for the first 20 days, but for the next 80 days you may be required to pay $10.50 per day, with Medicare paying the balance.

Medicare, after a stay in a hospital, also pays

for up to 100 home help visits from a participating home help agency, such as visiting nurses.

Medicare hospital insurance does not require any payment by individuals receiving retirement benefits.

You may also choose to be covered by the voluntary medical insurance (Medicaid). This covers visits to physicians and for many types of services by a hospital as an out-patient, such as skilled nursing services, or visits by a home help agency. You pay the first $60 of the cost each year and the medical insurance pays for 80 percent of the "reasonable charges" for other covered services. Medical insurance costs $6.70 each month; you may ask that the premiums be deducted from your monthly Social Security payments.

If you are not eligible for retirement benefits, you may still be eligible for Medicare hospital and medical insurance, for a cost of $36 per month for both plans.

Pensions and retirement plans

An employer is not required to provide a pension plan. However, if there is a pension plan, the federal Pension Reform Act of 1974, plus Internal Revenue Service requirements, must be met. If an employer has a pension plan, it is usually "qualified" or approved by the Internal Revenue Service so that the employer may deduct payments he makes and employees will not be required to pay taxes on contribu tions made by or for them at the time those contributions are made. The Internal Revenue Service rules help protect employees against any favoritism in the plan by giving substantially better treatment to higher paid company officials than to rank and file employees.

Individual retirement account

The federal Pension Reform Act permits an employee or management official, whether paid wages or a salary, to have an individual retirement account (IRA) if he is not covered by any other pension plan. This is a simple plan which lets an employee set aside money each year for retirement, and the amount he sets aside is not taxed as income. An employee may fill out a simple form with any savings bank, regular bank, insurance company, stock broker, or other investment agency, and pay into a fund in the employee's name up to 15 percent of his annual earnings, to $1,500 each year. The employee will normally not be taxed for interest earnings in his account until he is ready for retirement. If an employee changes jobs he may continue to pay into his personal IRA, so long as payments are not made for him to another retirement plan.

Self-employed persons

Self-employed individuals may establish a "Keough" plan in which they also make payments of up to 15 percent of their earnings with a maximum of $7,500 each year to a savings or investment account. Income tax is not required on the payments at the time of the payments. Interest or other earnings in an individual's account are usually not taxable until he is eligible to retire at age $59\frac{1}{2}$ or more.

A profit sharing plan is often established by an employer to pay a stated percentage of the employer's profit each year into a fund to be distributed to participating employees. If there are no profits, there are no contributions for that year. The profits are paid and distributed to accounts of individual employees on the basis of a formula, such as in direct portion to the salary paid. For example, if an employee is paid a higher wage rate, then a higher contribution is made on his behalf. In general, profit sharing plans appeal to younger employees, while pension plans appeal more to older employees.

Profit sharing

A pension plan or retirement plan is a program for the payment of benefits to eligible employees after their retirement. It may also include benefits payable upon death, benefits to the widow or widower of the covered employee, or payments to other dependents, or when disabled.

Types of pension plans

A fixed benefit pension plan is a pension plan in which the benefit upon retirement can be determined by a plan formula. Plan formulas are usually based upon the number of years of service of an employee under the plan and his earnings. Most plans negotiated by labor unions are a fixed benefit pension plan.

A money purchase pension plan is a plan in which the annual contribution to an employee's account is fixed or definitely determinable, but the future pension he may receive is not definitely fixed. The amount an employee will receive is based in large part upon the earnings of the assets (stocks, bonds, real estate property, etc.) owned by the plan.

Some plans provide that an employee have a stated number of units of all the assets of the pension plan, and when eligible to retire he has a lump sum portion of all of the plan's assets at that time. The plan may buy for a retiring employee an "annuity" with that money and pay to him each month a stated amount, based upon the earnings on the amount in his account and his anticipated life expectancy.

Other provisions

Most pension plans have a stated normal retirement age, such as age 65. Some plans permit early retirement, with reduced benefits. Other plans permit an employee to work and to make contributions after age 65, with additional or increased benefits. Many plans are "integrated" with the federal Social Security, so that a retired person may not receive more than a maximum percentage of his regular earnings upon retirement from both Social Security and the retirement plan. If Social Security benefits are increased then the pension plan pays less.

In some plans the employer pays all of the contributions, while in others the employer pays a portion and the balance is deducted from the employee's pay. Some plans permit an employee to pay an additional amount such as 2 percent, 6 percent, or 10 percent to his account. This contribution is a form of savings that are tax free to the employee until he withdraws the benefits, probably upon retirement.

Many pension plans and profit sharing plans

are operated by a legal trust, with trustees elected or appointed. The trustees usually hire an administrator and clerical employees. Sometimes there are separate trustees for the administration and investment of the assets owned by the plan, and for determining whether an individual is eligible for retirement or other benefits under the plan.

The federal Pension Reform Act of 1974 has strict requirements for employees who may "participate" in a pension plan. For example, if you are age 25 and have one year of service with the employer you must be granted one year of service. In general you will be credited for a year of service in any year in which you worked 1,000 hours or more.

Pension Reform Act

The Pension Reform Act also requires that contributions paid by an employer on behalf of an employee must be "vested" in his account so that they cannot be taken away. The law permits a pension plan to have three different formulas to choose from in order to vest the contributions: (1) full vesting after 10 years service or (2) after five years of service contributions must be 25 percent vested, 5 percent more for each of the next five years, and 10 percent more for the next five years until they are fully vested after fifteen years or (3) when an employee's age and his years of service total to 45, his benefits must begin to vest, provided that he has at least five years of service with the employer; his contributions must be 50 percent vested after ten years of service, and fully vested after 15 years of service.

The Pension Reform Act gives certain rights to "participants" (employees covered by a plan) in a profit sharing or pension plan. They include the following rights:

A written explanation of the plan revised at least once every five years if there are any amendments, to be given within 90 days after becoming eligible as a participant or beneficiary under the plan.

To be informed of a "material" change in the plan within 210 days after the end of the "plan year." To receive parts of the plan's annual report.

To see the plan documents such as the trust agreement or financial statements in the plan's office and to buy copies of those documents.

To receive, once a year, or upon leaving an employer covered by the plan, a statement as to your accrued benefits and how much is vested in your account.

To be told of a "break in service" when, for example, you were not paid the minimum number of hours required by the plan to maintain a continuity in your service.

To receive a statement of vested benefits when leaving the employer covered by the plan.

A participant in a pension plan can sue the trust administrators or trustees in federal court for violation of federal law and probably for violation of a provision in the trust agreement.

Part of the Pension Reform Act is enforced by the United States Department of Labor, Office of Welfare and Pension Reports. An individual may phone or write this office in a nearby city for information, or to ask that an investigation be made of a pension plan he believes is refusing to meet the requirements of the federal law.

Federal income tax deductions for employees

If an employee itemizes his federal income tax deduction each year rather than taking the standard deduction, he is entitled to many deductions for costs related to his employment. For example, an employee may deduct the cost of union dues, uniforms and required special work clothing, the expenses of travel, meals, and lodging while away from home in performance of services as an employee, other expenses related to work to the extent they are covered by a reimbursement or expense allowance arrangement with his employer, business transportation expenses other than cost of traveling to and from work, business gifts, and moving expenses he incurs to change to a job at least 50 miles farther than the distance between his old job and his former home. If an employee uses his car in connection with the employer's business, he may deduct either 15 cents per business mile, or the total expenses of his car, including depreciation, if he uses it only for business. If he uses it partly for business and partly for personal use, he may deduct a percentage of total costs.

An outside sales person may deduct from "gross income" the expenses in soliciting business for his employer away from the employer's place of business, whether or not the sales person itemizes deductions.

An employee must have documentary evidence for any lodging expense while traveling away from home and for any other expenditure of $25 or more.

Home office

If an employee uses part of his home for a business purpose, he may deduct part of the expense of maintaining his home. For example, if an employee uses one-half of a room only for office work connected with his employment and he has a five room home, he could probably deduct one-tenth of the cost of operating his home (mortgage interest payments, heat, electricity, telephone, real estate taxes, depreciation, etc.). He may be permitted to deduct only a pro rata tenth of the cost of his home.

If the employee uses a portion of the room ten hours a week he may not be permitted to deduct the entire amount. An employee may be required to show either that his employer requires that he have an office at home, or that there is a business reason for an office at home. Check with your tax consultant for the current status of employee business expense.

Records

An employee should keep accurate daily written records of all expenses incurred as an employee. He may have to prove to the Internal Revenue Service that he had these expenses. Keep the written documents for at least three years.

If an employee entertains clients or potential clients in connection with his employer's business, he should keep written records showing the amount of the expense, the time and place, that it had a business purpose, and the business relationship of the entertained person.

Moving expenses

Deductible moving expenses include the cost of transporting the employee and members of his household from the old to the new residence, the cost of transporting his household goods and personal effects, the cost of meals and lodging on the trip, and temporary living expenses for up to 30 days at a new job location. An employee may deduct expenses of traveling, including meals and lodging, from his former home to the general location of his new place of work for the principal purpose of looking for a new home. Expenses incident to a sale, purchase, or a lease including real estate commission fees and some loan charges, are usually deductible. An employee must report payments received from an employer for moving expenses.

If an employee, male or female, maintains a household he may deduct at least part of the expense of taking care of a dependent under age 15 or a mentally or physically ill dependent. The maximum deduction is $400 per month. The amount that can be deducted is reduced for employees with a higher income.

Certain income indirectly connected with his employment is not taxable to an employee. For example, unemployment compensation received from the state employment office is not taxable income. Likewise, retirement benefits received from Social Security are not taxable income. Disability benefits are not usually taxable whether from Social Security, Workman's Compensation, or a private insurance plan for which the employee paid the premium.

Non-taxable income

If an employee receives strike benefits from a union the payments are probably taxable if the employee was expected to perform any services, such as picket duty, in return for the benefits or as a condition of obtaining those strike benefits. Back pay received from an employer as a result of action by the National Labor Relations Board or the U.S. Department of Labor, is taxable income.

Sick pay

If the employer pays an employee when he is absent due to sickness or injury, it will probably be reported as income. An employee may on his income tax return deduct this up to 75 dollars a week for the first 30 days, if his regular weekly earnings are at least $100. After 30 days he may deduct up to $100 a week. If an employee receives sickness or injury payments from a fund or insurance plan paid for in part by his employer, only the portion paid for by the employer can be treated as tax-free sick pay.

Consult your tax consultant for answers for specific tax problems since the law changes fast in this area.

part three

What you should know about unions

How a union is organized

The National Labor Relations Act, the federal Railway Labor Act, state labor relations acts in many states, and court decisions often protect the right of an individual employee or a group of employees to form and join a "labor organization," commonly called a union.

If employees are not represented by any labor union some employees may desire to organize their own union or to talk with agents of existing unions.

Unions are more successful in organizing where employees are not satisfied. The employees may believe that their employer pays lower wages than a competitor or lower wages than others in their area. Some employees may organize to get a "better" pension plan or health and welfare plan. Sometimes morale is low among employees because of too much overtime or too little work, or because of acts by management that employees believe to be arbitrary.

In the past, most labor unions tended to limit themselves to representing employees in a particular industry or to employees performing a particular type of work. In the past few years, however, many unions have been willing to represent many types of employees working for a broad range of employers.

Most union organizers will be glad to talk with an employee, or to meet with any employees. The organizer will probably meet with employees at the union office or in a private home, usually in the evening. In the meeting he will probably explain the procedure used by his union—how authorization cards or applications for membership in the union would be used, the procedure for getting recognition from the employer if enough employees are interested in that union, and the procedure in negotiating a collective bargaining agreement. He will probably pass out authorization cards, usually 3 x 5 inches in size, to employees and ask that they sign them.

The organizer will request that each employee present ask other employees to sign a card and return it to him or to one of the "key" employees helping him. The cards should not be signed on company property during working time, but they could be signed in nonworking areas during nonworking time such as coffee breaks or the lunch period. Some supervisors do not like any talk about a union and they may ask questions to determine who is trying to bring the union in. Many organizers tell employees not to discuss their organizing efforts with supervisors, or to let them know that there is interest in organizing a union.

If employees want to organize an "independent union" and not be subject to control by outsiders they can prepare authorization cards by printing them on a mimeograph machine or similar process. A model authorization card that could be used for an election or to seek recognition without an election appears in Appendix E. Or an employee can prepare a petition such as the following for any union, including an "independent union" employees want to establish:

> We, the undersigned employees of John Doe Company, desire that the National Labor Relations Board conduct an election to determine if the John Doe Employee Union should be our exclusive bargaining representative.
>
> Signature: Date:

If employees organize an "independent" or "company" union they should choose a name and select a committee of fellow employees to establish a constitution and bylaws. They will want to decide what offices the union has, how officers are selected, the length of their terms, the amount of initiation fees and dues, when meetings will be held, and so forth. An employer and his supervisors should not participate in forming or operating a union, for they may be charged with an unfair labor practice.

If the union is recognized by an employer as the exclusive bargaining representative, whether or not it has won an election, the union must meet certain requirements of the federal Labor-Management Reporting and Disclosure Act of

1959 (Landrum–Griffin Act). Within 90 days after recognition by an employer the union must file a report with the U.S. Department of Labor, Office of Labor-Management and Welfare-Pension Reports (LMWP). A union must adopt a constitution and bylaws and two copies must be filed with a report, Form LM-1. A union is required to list names of its officers, initiation and other fees, regular dues and other periodic payments required of members, and information such as:

1. Restrictions on membership.
2. How to participate in insurance or other benefit plans.
3. How disbursement of union funds is authorized.
4. How meetings are called.
5. How officers and others are selected or disciplined.
6. How fines or discipline of members are handled.
7. How hearings and appeals are handled.
8. How bargaining demands and strikes are authorized.
9. How contract terms are ratified.
10. How work permits are issued.

The annual financial report requires listing of (*a*) assets and debts owed at the beginning and end of the year, (*b*) receipts and where they came from, (*c*) salaries and payments to officers and employees, (*d*) money paid out, (*e*) loans to any business, and (*f*) loans that totaled $250 or more in a year to any officer, employee, or member.

If the total value of the property and yearly receipts of the union is more than $5,000, then a bond to protect against loss by fraud or dishonesty must cover each officer, agent, shop steward, representative, or employee of the union who handles union funds or other property.

The regional office of the LMWP can help an individual in filling out the reports, but they must be mailed to the Director, Office of Labor-Management Standards Enforcement, U.S. Department of Labor, 200 Constitution Avenue, Washington, D.C. 20216.

Employees should not get signatures of other employees during working time. Soliciting signatures for the petition or cards can be prohibited in work areas, if the employer prohibits solicitations for charity fund drives or other groups. A foreman who may be a true "supervisor" rather than just a leadman or "straw boss" should not sign.

Getting signatures

When 30 percent or more of the employees in an "appropriate bargaining unit" sign cards for the union it may send those cards or a petition with a "Petition" for an election form to a regional office of the National Labor Relations Board. The NLRB will then send a copy of that petition to the employer.

The NLRB will not order an employer to bargain with a union unless the union claims to represent all employees in "an appropriate bargaining unit." Likewise, the NLRB will not con-

The appropriate bargaining unit

duct an election unless it covers employees in an appropriate voting unit. Many bargaining units cover "all production and maintenance employees." Some units, however, may include only a particular group of employees, who have a different type of work or hours, or working conditions much different from other employees, and who have separate supervision or a separate work location.

Some groups of employees that may be permitted to have a separate unit include truck drivers, warehouse employees, salesmen, laboratory employees, and maintenance employees in a "true craft unit" that usually requires an apprentice training period. Office clerical employees and professional employees (such as engineers, usually required to have an engineering degree) are excluded from an overall production and maintenance unit in most cases. Guards, watchmen, and supervisors are excluded in all cases. A "supervisor" is more than a leadman or "straw boss" but he is not required to have authority to hire or fire.

If an employer has several locations, each plant or store may be an appropriate unit. The NLRB usually "presumes" that a single plant or store can be an appropriate unit. However, if they are only a few miles apart, there is some transfer of employees from one location to another, and most management decisions are made at another location, then the NLRB may find that a separate unit is not appropriate. An individual can phone or visit the NLRB regional office near-

est him for information about the appropriate
unit.

A union cannot be effective in getting improved wages, hours, and working conditions unless it is recognized by the employer as the "exclusive" bargaining representative for employees. (However, some laws covering government
employees permit a union to represent and sign
a contract only for its members.) A union that
has authorization cards from over half of the
employees in a bargaining unit will frequently
write a letter to the employer requesting that it
be recognized and that the employer meet with it
to bargain for a contract.

Getting
recognition
from the
employer

Many employers will not accept such a statement and will either insist upon an NLRB election or other proof that the union represents the
employees. Sometimes there is a "card check"
by a neutral person such as the State Department of Labor. This card check consists of a
comparison of the names and, perhaps, also the
signatures on the authorization cards with a list
of names submitted by the employer, and perhaps also the signatures of employees from the
employer's payroll records. The person con-
ducting the card check will then certify whether
the union represents a majority of the employees, based upon the authorization cards.

Sometimes an employer will not agree to a
card check or with the results of a card check,
and he will refuse to agree to recognize the union unless it wins an election. The NLRB usually
upholds the right of an employer to insist that

the union win an election. But if the employer commits "serious" unfair labor practices (such as threats to fire employees who support the union, or to close his business if the union wins), then the NLRB may, after an unfair labor charge is filed and a trial is conducted, order the employer to bargain with the union without an election, if it had authorization cards from a majority of the employees.

Sometimes the employer has reason to doubt that the employees who signed an authorization card really want the union to represent them. For example, there may be organizing activity by two or more unions and the same employee may sign an authorization card for each union. Sometimes a union organizer tells employees that the card is to be used only to get an NLRB election and says nothing about the possibility that the card may be used to seek recognition by the employer without an election. Sometimes the language on the cards is so confusing that the card does not clearly authorize the union to represent that employee for the purposes of bargaining with the employer. The union may request recognition in a bargaining unit the employer believes is not appropriate. For example, the union may seek recognition in one department, and the employer may contend that only a unit of all employees would be appropriate. In all of those cases the NLRB may not order the employer to bargain with a union, even though it had cards from most of the employees. In any of these situations the employer may insist that the union file a petition for an NLRB election, or the employer may file a petition for an election.

National Labor Relations Board election procedure

If an employee wants the NLRB to conduct an election he must complete the NLRB's "Petition" form, sign it, and send it to the NLRB regional office nearest him. The NLRB regional office will send him copies of their petition form and their agents will help him complete the form if the employee should ask them for help. There is no fee for this service. If an employee prefers, he may consult a private attorney to assist him, and he will be expected to pay the attorney's usual fee. A list of addresses and phone numbers of the NLRB regional offices appears in Appendix B and a completed copy of the NLRB petition appears in Appendix G.

Within 48 hours after filing the petition, but preferably with the petition, an individual or a union must also send to the NLRB proof that at least 30 percent of the employees in the proposed bargaining unit want the election. This could be union authorization cards recently dated and signed by the employees.

The NLRB will not conduct an election or handle an unfair labor practice matter unless the employer involved meets the "jurisdictional standards" of the NLRB. A retail business must have gross sales of at least $500,000 a year to meet these standards. A non-retail business, such as a warehouse, factory, or contractor, in general, must either buy $50,000 a year worth of

Petition form

NLRB dollar jurisdiction requirements

products from outside the state, or sell $50,000 worth outside the state, or do that much business a year with customers who do. Railroads and interstate airlines are covered by the Railway Labor Act (see Part Five [Summary of federal and state agencies: Railway Labor Act]), not by the NLRB.

For a case against a union, the NLRB usually looks at the volume of business done by an employer involved in the matter against the union. For example, if the charge is that a union is not fairly operating a hiring hall, look for the business volume done by any employer who has an agreement to hire employees from that hall.

The NLRB regional office can advise the employee of its jurisdictional standards.

Decertification elections

If employees want to get rid of a union they do not like, any employee in the unit represented by the union may file a petition to "decertify" the union. See Appendix F for a sample NLRB petition form. With the election petition or within 48 hours, the "petitioner" must send to the NLRB office recently signed and dated signatures from 30 percent or more of the employees in the bargaining unit. One way to obtain this "showing of interest" is for an employee to prepare a heading such as the following on a sheet of paper:

We, the undersigned employees of _____ _____ Company, desire that the National Labor Relations Board conduct an election to determine whether the _____ _____ Union continues to represent the employees.
Signature: Date:

An employee should not circulate that petition for signatures in working areas during paid time, but he may circulate it during coffee breaks or during lunch periods, or before or after working hours. Do not get signatures of supervisors, and do not get prior approval of management before circulating the petition, since the union may claim that the employer has given unlawful assistance to the employee, and the NLRB may not conduct the election.

On the NLRB petition form under "Unit Involved" the petitioner should state the existing bargaining unit. If he does not know this and there is a recent collective bargaining agreement he can copy the job classifications listed there as "Included" and list the usual exclusions (guards and supervisors). One may phone or write to the nearest NLRB regional office to answer other questions about how to get an election. (Note: the bylaws of some unions provide that a member may be fined by the union if he files a petition to decertify the union. If the union threatens to fine an employee for this reason it is an unfair labor practice; notify the NLRB.)

If an employee cannot file a petition to decertify the union because an election is "barred" by a contract, but he does not want to continue to pay dues or fees to the union, he can file for a "union security de-authorization election." Union security includes a contract requirement that employees join the union after 30 days (or after 7 days in the construction industry) or pay fees to the union. To get the election an individual must obtain signatures from 30 percent of the employees as stated above under "Decer-

Union security elections

tification Elections." An employer cannot ask for this kind of election. On a sheet of paper an employee could prepare a heading such as the following:

We, the undersigned employees of _____.
_____ Company, desire that the National Labor Relations Board conduct an election to determine whether the union security clause, section _____ in the collective bargaining agreement, should be removed.
Signature: Date:

In the NLRB petition form list the bargaining unit as provided above. The "petitioner" should also send to the NLRB a copy of the current bargaining agreement or the recently expired agreement, and mark the union shop, the agency shop, union dues check-off, or other form of union security in the contract. If, in the election, a majority of the employees vote to remove the union security provisions of the contract, the NLRB will certify that the union security provisions are no longer effective. The remaining portion of the contract will remain in effect, but the union cannot then request the employer to fire anyone because he has not paid dues or initiation or other fees.

An employer may petition for an election

Where a union makes a claim upon the employer that it represents the employees, the employer may itself file a petition for an election with the NLRB. The employer may also petition for an election if he believes that the union with which he has been dealing no longer represents the employees, but with this petition he must sign a letter stating what facts cause him to doubt that the union represents his employees.

An employee should send an original and about three copies of the signed, completed petition form to the nearest NLRB regional office. One copy of the sheet with employee signatures, or of authorization cards, will be enough. The NLRB will "docket" the petition as a "case," assign it to a field examiner or attorney in the regional office and will send a copy of the petition to the company and to the union, if any. With the petition to the company, the NLRB will send a copy of a "Notice to Employees" form advising of the filing of the petition and of rights of employees, and ask that it be posted. The NLRB will also send to the company a form requesting information to determine if the NLRB has "jurisdiction" over the company.

The NLRB will not usually conduct an election if there is a collective bargaining agreement currently in effect. This is called the "contract bar rule." However, the NLRB will accept the filing of an election petition in the 30-day period beginning 90 days and ending 60 days before the contract's expiration or "automatic renewal" date. If the contract has been in effect at least two years and nine months, the NLRB will accept the filing of a petition by employees or a petition by a rival union, even though the contract by its terms still has another year or more to run. In a "health care institution" the petition should be filed in the period 120 to 90 days before the expiration date.

The NLRB will not conduct an election for a

What the NLRB will do with the petition

full year after any prior "valid" NLRB election in that voting unit.

Agreements for an election

If the employer and the union and any other party "consent" to an election, the NLRB will probably ask them to sign a standard NLRB form agreeing that the regional director of the NLRB may resolve any disagreement as to whether there was improper conduct by either of them before the election, or whether particular individuals were eligible to vote. If an individual signs this kind of form, his right to appeal any action of the regional director is very limited.

Another type of NLRB form provides that the parties "stipulate" that if there are disagreements as to whether there was improper conduct or whether particular individuals were eligible to vote, that the regional director only makes an investigation and a report for the Board, which resolves the dispute.

Hearing to determine if election should be directed

If the parties do not sign an election agreement, the regional director will probably direct that a hearing be conducted to determine if there should be an election. That hearing is normally scheduled in the city where the employer's business is located, a few weeks after the petition is filed. Presiding at this hearing will be a hearing officer from the NLRB regional office; a court reporter will record what is said and later will type a transcript. If an individual files the election petition, he will probably want to be represented by an attorney. However, the hearing officer will assist him in seeing that an adequate record is made to resolve properly the issues in the case.

The hearing officer will ask the employer, the union, and any other party to enter into certain stipulations of fact and law. Among those are the type of and amount of business done by the employer, that the union is a "labor organization," that the filing of the petition raised a "question concerning representation," the history of bargaining by the employer with any union, and on the employees that should be included and excluded from the bargaining unit. Witnesses will then testify and exhibits will be received as evidence.

A month or so after the hearing closes, the regional director usually issues a written decision, either dismissing the petition, or directing that an election be conducted in a particular unit of employees. He sends a copy of his decision to all parties to the hearing.

Decision of NLRB regional director

If the union and the employer consent to an election or if the NLRB directs that an election be conducted, the employer will be asked within seven days to file with the NLRB an election "eligibility list" of those employees who can vote in the election. The NLRB will send a copy of this list (often called the "Excelsior list," named for the case where the NLRB first issued this requirement) with names and the home addresses to all other "parties" to the election. The other parties may then use this list to send election campaign literature.

Election eligibility list

Before any NLRB election there is usually campaign propaganda put out by the union and the employer. Campaigns before an NLRB election are somewhat similar to campaigns before any national or state election.

Election campaign propaganda and meetings

The union usually promises that if employees select the union that it will negotiate a collective bargaining agreement for them similar to agreements it or other locals of the union have negotiated with other employers. The union usually promises a wage increase, better health and welfare or pension benefits, and protection for employees against arbitrary action by the employer. Unions often try to convince employees that the employer will cheat them in every way he can, and employees need this union to protect themselves.

The employer usually states that employees presently enjoy wages and other benefits equal to that existing in other companies that have a union; that the union cannot promise and guarantee employees anything; if the union wins an election the employer will bargain in good faith but neither the union, the NLRB nor anyone else can force him to agree to anything. An employer may state that if he does not agree to union demands it may force the employees to strike, in which case the employees would not have any earnings and the employer could permanently replace them with new hires. The employer will point out (except in states with a "right to work law") that if the employees select a union, the union may negotiate a contract requiring all employees to join the union and pay monthly dues of a certain amount each month and that an employee who does not join the union will have to be fired and the union can fine employees if they violate the union's rules.

The union agents can meet with employees at

their homes and attempt to get their support. The NLRB usually rules that it is not proper for an employer or supervisors to follow a practice of visiting employees in their homes to try to convince them not to support the union.

Supervisors and other employer officials may state their opinion to employees about the union in the location where employees work, or in a meeting with a group of employees.

If an employer holds a "captive audience" meeting with employees during paid time to discuss the union, the union may request a similar meeting to reply. It may not be entitled to such a meeting if it can talk with a large portion of the employees during lunch or rest periods or in their homes or other places.

Over the years the NLRB has developed for its elections rules that are usually considered to provide for a fair election. The procedure varies slightly among the NLRB regions, but the procedure is substantially as given below:

Voting in NLRB elections

A few days before the scheduled time of the election, the employer should post on the bulletin board the NLRB's "Notice of Election" form, which states the voting unit, the date, time and place of election, and also a sample of the NLRB's secret ballot.

About half an hour or more before the time that balloting is scheduled to begin, the party who filed the petition (petitioner), the union(s), and the employer agents meet with the NLRB agent. He will ask the employer, union, and other parties to select one or more observers to help him to conduct the election. It is not necessary that any party have an observer, but he may if he wishes. An observer cannot be a full-time agent of the union or a supervisor or other agent for the employer. In this "preelection conference," the NLRB agent will explain the voting procedure and the parties will then inspect the voting area.

Shortly before the opening of the polls, the NLRB agent and any observers will have before them the list of eligible voters received from the employer. This usually lists employees who are on the payroll in a job in the bargaining unit during the payroll period that ended just before the election was directed or consented to. When the balloting begins each voter states his name to the NLRB agent. The observers check his name on the eligibility list, and the NLRB agent hands the voter a ballot. The voter then takes it to the nearby hidden area, such as an adjoining room or a booth, marks it, folds it and puts it into the ballot box and leaves the voting area.

In some elections there may be several voting periods. After each period the ballot box is sealed by closing the slot with tape and by writing signatures across the tape.

At the close of the balloting the polls are closed and the union, employer, and other parties are called back into the area for the count. The NLRB agent prepares a "Certification on Conduct of Election" form and asks the observers to sign it, certifying that all eligible voters had a chance to vote in secret. A party may later file objections to the election even though his observer signed this form.

Before the count is begun the NLRB agent at-

tempts to get the parties to agree whether individuals whose ballot was challenged had the
right to vote. Then the NLRB agent counts the
ballots, with the parties observing. At the end
of the count the NLRB agent prepares a "Tally
of Ballots" and gives a copy to each party.

A sample ballot where only one union seeks
recognition is included in Appendix D. The ballot used where two or more unions are competing is similar, but it also has a block for "Neither."

A union must have a majority of the valid
votes cast to be certified as the exclusive bargaining representative of employees in the voting
unit.

If there are two or more choices such as "no,"
and two or more unions, but no choice receives a
majority, a runoff election may be scheduled between the two choices which receive the greatest
number of votes. Those eligible to vote in the
runoff election will be those employees who
were eligible to vote in the first election, provided that they are still employed in the voting
unit as of the date of the runoff election. Employees new to the voting unit will not be permitted to vote in the runoff.

Sometimes the NLRB will conduct an election
by mail ballot or a combination of mail ballot
and manual voting. Mail ballots are sent from
the NLRB regional office to the homes of voters
a week or more before the count. Instructions
are sent with each ballot. A notice of election is
posted at the employer's premises and the employees are informed that if they do not receive
a ballot by a certain date they should im-

Mail ballot
elections

mediately ask the NLRB for a copy if they believe they are eligible to vote. If an individual
filed the petition and believed that someone may
vote who he believes not to be eligible to vote,
he should phone or write a note to the NLRB
agent stating that he wants to challenge that person's vote, and the reason for the challenge. The
parties are notified that they may be present for
the count, at a stated time and place, usually in
the regional office of the NLRB.

Challenged ballots and objections

If the number of challenged ballots that are
not resolved could affect the outcome of the
election then the election is usually not final until the NLRB rules on whether each individual
whose ballot was challenged had a right to vote.

Within five working days, beginning the first
day after the election and ending at the close of
business of the fifth day, any party may file objections to the conduct of the election. Objections
must be post-marked before midnight. Four copies must be mailed to the NLRB regional office
and a statement added such as the following:

> I hereby certify that on this date I served a copy
> of the above objections upon (names and ad-
> dresses of all other parties, such as the employer
> and the unions or petitioner) by depositing in the
> U.S. mail a postage prepaid copy addressed to
> each of the above parties.
> Signed this _____ day of _____, 19_____.

The objections must state exactly what you
think another party did which was wrong and
which interfered with the conduct of the election,
or the right of employees to express their free
choice. One may object to any conduct of an-

other party that occurred after the petition for election was filed with the NLRB.

If the employer before an election, promised a new benefit to employees or an improved benefit, or if he threatens the loss of an existing benefit, it may be grounds for filing objections. If the employer or union makes a statement to employees that seriously misrepresents the facts, it is also objectionable.

If objections are filed to the election or if the challenged ballots could affect the outcome, the NLRB agent usually conducts an investigation to determine the facts. He will ask the parties to provide witnesses to help him determine the facts. Sometimes in a close case or where he is unable to determine the facts because of conflicting versions of what happened, the regional director may schedule a hearing on objections or challenged ballots. This is a formal hearing at which a hearing officer, usually from the NLRB regional office, will participate, witnesses will be called to testify, and a court reporter will take down their testimony. It will be conducted somewhat like a court trial but it is less formal. If an individual files the petition in the matter, he may desire to be represented by an attorney, in which case the individual will be expected to make a complete record.

After the hearing closes the hearing officer will prepare a lengthy report finding facts and analyzing the law, and include a recommendation. Copies will be served upon all parties to the proceeding. The decision of the hearing officer may be appealed either to the regional director or to the Board. The report will inform the parties of the procedure used to appeal.

Employees out on an economic strike (a strike seeking higher wages, better hours, or working conditions, and not caused or prolonged by a "serious" unfair labor practice by the employer) may vote in an election even though they are permanently replaced. Their replacements are also eligible to vote in the election. However, if the strike began more than 12 months before the date of the election, strikers are usually not eligible to vote.

Certification

If no objections are filed in the five-day period after balloting, and if challenged ballots would not change the outcome of the election, the NLRB regional office issues a document. It certifies either that the union is the bargaining representative or that the union lost.

If objections to the election are filed within the five days, the NLRB investigates them and if they are found to have merit it conducts another election. If challenged ballots could determine the outcome of the election, the NLRB investigates them and rules on whether the individuals were eligible to vote. If the NLRB finds them to be eligible it opens the challenge ballot envelope for each eligible employee, counts the ballots, and certifies whether the union won.

If a union is recognized

Early negotiation procedure

If the employer recognizes a union as representing a group of employees, the union will attempt to get the employer to agree upon a collective bargaining agreement, usually called a contract. The usual procedure is for the union to present a complete written proposal to the employer, based upon contracts which the union has with other employers in the industry. Other more democratic unions hold meetings with employees to determine what they want to ask for. In general, there is no law that requires a union to get the ideas of the employees before making a proposal to an employer. However, if the employees are not satisfied with the representation given to them by the union they could vote to decertify the union in an NLRB election, or they can in the next election of union officers vote out the present officers and elect new officers. If the union's constitution and by-laws require a particular procedure to be followed before submitting proposals to an employer, then an individual member or members could enforce that provision. If the constitution and by-laws provide an appeal procedure from the action or failure to act by the union agents or officers, then that procedure should be followed, at least for up to four months. As a rule courts will not accept a lawsuit to enforce a union constitution or by-laws until a member has attempted to "exhaust" or use up his appeal procedures within the union, provided they do not require longer than four months.

The union usually asks the employer for a meeting to discuss its proposal. Many employers present a complete counter proposal of a contract, using the employer's language, including only provisions that the employer is willing to

agree to. Other employers are willing to negotiate from the union's proposal.

Some unions do not have any provision for an
employee negotiating or bargaining committee,
but use only paid professional negotiators to
represent the union.

**Coverage of
union contracts**
Collective bargaining agreements vary considerably from one union to another and from
one industry or type of work covered to another.
Some contracts are typically long and others are
only two or three pages long. In some industries
the union negotiates a "standard" or "area" contract and is usually successful at getting all employers whose employees are represented by the
union to sign a copy of that contract. These industries include construction, longshoring, retail
stores, trucking, and railroads.

In many industries, groups of employers bargain together with the union in an employer association. When a contract is agreed upon it applies to all employers in that bargaining unit.
Such a group of employers or association is
treated as a "single employer" for many purposes. For example, if a rival union wants to
represent some of those employees, it may be required to ask the NLRB for an election among
the employees of all the employers in the bargaining unit.

A typical union contract includes the names
of the union and employer covered by it. The
"recognition clause" states the employees covered by the contract and those excluded. A "union security clause" may require payment of
dues or membership in the union to keep em-

ployment. Other common provisions are a grievance and arbitration procedure; the procedure
used in obtaining promotions or in layoffs and
recalls such as the use of seniority and ability;
the classification of employees such as regular,
temporary, probationary, seasonal, part-time, or
casual; provisions dealing with the sub-contract-
ing of work and whether employees not in the
bargaining unit may perform "unit" work; a
no-strike, no-lockout clause; definitions of work
day, work week, overtime and premium pay,
call-in or reporting pay; holiday pay and recognized holidays, various work rules such as
safety; lunch and rest periods; vacations; hospital insurance, other insurance plans, pension
plan; length of the contract and the date when it
can be terminated or "opened" for further negotiations; wage rates for various job classifications, etc.

Union security includes any requirement in   **Union security**
the contract between the employer and the union
that requires employees to pay a sum of money
or to become a member of the union to maintain
their employment. A "closed shop" requires an
employee to be a member of the union before he
can be hired. A closed shop is unlawful under
federal labor laws and is also unlawful in most
states.

A "union shop" requires membership in the
union in good standing after a period of time.
Federal law permits a contract requirement that
an individual become a member after 30 days'
employment, but this is after only 7 days in the
construction industry.

Many courts have interpreted the union shop to require only the payment of a regular initiation fee and periodic dues, usually each month, to the union. Courts and federal and state labor agencies usually do not require any employee to become a "full member" of a union to maintain his job. An employee cannot, as a general rule, be required to take an oath of allegiance to the constitution and bylaws of the union or to sign an application for membership in a union.

If an employee offers to pay periodic dues and the initiation fee but refuses to become a full member in the union and the union requests his employer to terminate the employee for not being a "member in good standing," the employee can go to the NLRB to file an unfair labor practice charge against the union. A union cannot require that an employee pay dues for a period of time prior to his employment with the current employer.

A union cannot require that an employee pay a fine or assessment as a condition of keeping his job. However, if the union used the procedure set out in its own constitution and bylaws to assess and levy that fine or assessment against a member, it can probably go to court to collect that fine or assessment, or it can terminate his membership in the union, or both. It cannot however, insist that the employer fire the employee, so long as he offers to pay the initiation fee and regular dues.

An agency shop requires that an employee pay a stated amount regularly, such as each month, to the union to maintain employment, but membership is not required.

A "grandfather clause" permits employees who are working for the employer at a particular date to continue to refuse to pay union initiation fees or dues, but new employees hired after that date may be required to pay such dues or fees.

A "maintenance of membership clause" requires members of the union to maintain their membership (continue to pay dues) during the term of the contract, or the union may insist that the employer fire them. However, such contracts usually have an "escape period" at the end of the contract that permits an employee to give written notice to the union and the employer to cancel his membership. If the employee meets the requirements of that clause he no longer has to pay union dues or fees.

Many contracts that have any form of "union security" also have a "dues check-off" which permits an employee to sign a written authorization to be given to the employer to authorize deductions for the initiation fee or dues from the employee's pay check each month. Thus the employer becomes the collection agent for the union.

If you live in one of the 19 states with a "right to work clause" it is probably unlawful for any contract requiring membership in or payment of dues or fees to the union to be enforced, either by the union or by the employer. If the union attempts to enforce such a clause an employee could go to the NLRB to file an unfair labor practice charge against the union. If the employer discharges an employee for failure to pay union dues or fees the employee could also file charges against the employer. If the NLRB finds a violation of its laws it will probably order the employee to be reinstated with payment of back pay.

Grievances

Nearly all union contracts have a procedure for handling disputes that arise during the term of the contract. Some contracts make any dispute that arises between an employee and the employer or between the union and the employer to be the subject of a grievance. Other contracts require an employer to discuss as a grievance only matters involving the interpretation or the application of the contract.

If there is a union that represents an employee and a complaint with the supervisor is not settled, the employee may notify the union. Many union contracts state the procedure that should be followed if a complaint, gripe, or grievance is not settled between an employee and his immediate supervisor. If employees take action, such as refusing to work or picketing, before their union has had time to attempt to settle the dispute, then the employer may not be required to even discuss the dispute with the employees, and they could be fired. For example, the United States Supreme Court ruled that an employer may discharge employees who picket to protest their employer's alleged discriminatory racial policies, when these employees could have waited for their union to process a grievance protesting those racial policies.

The procedure for handling a dispute varies, with some contracts providing for an elaborate procedure. At the first step the employee usually discusses the gripe or dispute with his immediate foreman. If he is not satisfied he may discuss his problem with a job steward (if the union has stewards), who is usually another employee. If there is no steward, the employee may discuss it with the union business agent, who is often a full-time, paid agent or officer of the union. If the steward or business agent believes the employee has a valid complaint, he will usually go with the complaining employee to discuss it with the next higher level of management.

In any discussion of a grievance, try to be sure of the "facts." If it involves a dispute over pay, for example, an employer may take the payroll records or an employee may take the paycheck stub for the last few pay periods with him. Each should take a copy of the contract. One should explain his position without arguing or losing patience. No one is always right. A grievance meeting should be mostly a discussion of the facts, at least at the first part of the meeting. The parties should see if they can agree on what happened. When they decide what happened, they should attempt to agree on the contract sections involved. The parties may still have an honest difference of opinion as to how the contract should be applied to the particular facts. See the discussion above at page 31, how to present a complaint to your employer.

If the employee still does not agree, the union may decide that there has been a violation of the contract, and will take it up to the next step in the grievance procedure. The dispute should be written, with the complaining employee stating his version of what happened that caused the dispute to arise, and the contract sections believed to have been violated. The steward or business agent, and the foreman or supervisor, should each write on the grievance form what was discussed in the grievance meeting.

Most contracts provide that a grievance must be filed within a stated time period, such as seven days, after the event occurred. The contract usually states a time period within which the grievance must be "appealed" to the next step. If it is not appealed within that period the right to appeal may have been lost. However, some courts and arbitrators rule that a grievance may still be heard if the complaining employee or the union was not careless in their delay, or if they were absent for a while, or if they did not know about the event that caused the dispute.

If a matter can be made the subject of a grievance, such as the employer refusing to pay the wage rate or hours an employee thinks is proper, the employee should go ahead and do the job assigned to him by the foreman. If the employee believes the foreman is wrong, the employee may, on time not paid for, consult the steward or the business agent to discuss whether to file a grievance. If an employee flatly refuses to do a job assigned to him, it might result in his being fired, even though the union believes that his interpretation of the contract is correct. Employees and the union should first do the job, then use the grievance procedure. If there is a strike or work stoppage over a matter that could be covered by a grievance, it may be an unlawful work stoppage.

An employee should not leave his work area during work time to investigate or get facts from other employees about a grievance, unless he has permission from his supervisor. Even if an employee has a valid grievance, but he abandons his job duties, he could properly be disciplined for that. Likewise, a union steward should not leave his work area to investigate a grievance or to attend a grievance hearing unless the contract clearly gives him that right, or unless he has permission from his immediate supervisor or the proper company official. Even if the contract gives a steward the right to leave his job duties to handle a grievance, the steward should first notify his immediate supervisor.

If a grievance is not settled satisfactorily to the union, most contracts provide that the union may take it to arbitration. Some contracts also permit the employer to take the dispute to arbitration. While a union has a duty to represent everyone fairly in the bargaining unit, whether a member of the union or not, and regardless of race or color, the union is not required to take a grievance to arbitration if the union agents in "good faith" believe there is little likelihood of winning before an arbitrator.

Arbitration is a procedure for a neutral person or persons to interpret or apply a contract to a particular situation, and the decision is usually binding on the employer and the union.

Arbitration

(Compare this with mediation, whether neither the employer nor the union is required to agree to suggestions of the mediator.)

The contract usually states how the arbitrator is selected. Most contracts provide for one neutral arbitrator, but some contracts also provide for equal numbers of one or two arbitrators for the employer and one or two for the union. Some contracts provide for a committee of employer and union representatives to issue a decision that can be binding on both sides. A few employers and unions that have a large number of arbitration cases agree to a "permanent" arbitrator or umpire for the duration of the contract.

The contract usually provides for selection of a neutral arbitrator, either from a list supplied by the Federal Mediation and Conciliation Service, a federal government agency, or by the American Arbitration Association, a private organization. When the arbitrator is selected, a hearing is scheduled before him. Sometimes the parties (usually the employer and the union) are each represented by an attorney and a court reporter is present to record everything that is said. Such a hearing is similar to a court trial, but is not as formal. The arbitrator usually permits witnesses to testify to matters and he will receive exhibits that a court would not permit. The main object of the arbitrator is to get the facts and apply the contract to those facts.

In the hearing the arbitrator usually attempts to get the parties to agree on exactly what the dispute is about, to agree to the contract sections that must be interpreted, and to agree to as many facts as they can. Evidence is received as to other grievances or arbitration decisions affecting the same section of the contract, what was said by the parties about the intent of those sections in grievance or other meetings, or in labor negotiations to change the language, and the "past practices" or how the employer has interpreted and applied that rule or contract section.

If briefs are permitted after the hearing, the parties may name and analyze decisions of the same arbitrator or other arbitrators interpreting similar rules or contract language. Decisions of arbitrators are published by several groups, including the Bureau of National Affairs and the American Arbitration Association. The bound or loose-leaf volumes may be found in a law library or in some city libraries.

An arbitrator has considerable authority to interpret and apply a contract to a particular situation, unless his authority is clearly limited by language in the contract or by a "stipulation" or other agreement by the parties. Employers and unions nearly always abide by the decision of an arbitrator, but his decision may be appealed to a court. The cost of arbitration, including the arbitrator's fee (about $200 a day), and the hearing room rental is usually shared equally by the employer and the union. Each side pays its own attorney's fee and the reporter's charge for the transcript.

If a dispute between a union and an employer may be taken to binding arbitration, a union cannot call or support a strike of employees on that matter. The union may take the matter to arbitration but cannot lawfully strike. Employees who strike may be terminated and the union can be sued by the employer for actual damages caused by the breach of contract, and the employer can ask a court to grant an injunction against the strike.

Court enforcement of collective bargaining agreements

A collective bargaining agreement is somewhat like any other contract. If there is a breach or violation of any of its terms the other party to the agreement—union or employer—may sue in court for breach of contract. However, if the contract has a clause providing for arbitration of any dispute over the interpretation of the contract, then a court will usually refuse to decide the dispute. A union and employer may be required to go to arbitration rather than to court.

If a union or employer refuses to use the procedure in the contract for arbitration, the other party may ask a court to order arbitration of the dispute. If a union or employer refuses to honor the decision of an arbitrator, the other party can ask a court for an order enforcing the arbitrator's award.

Federal law, as outlined in Section 301 of the National Labor Relations Act, as amended, must usually be followed in court actions to enforce a collective bargaining agreement. However, the lawsuit may be brought in a federal or a state court. Section 301 can also be used in a lawsuit over breach of an agreement by an employer to make payments to a labor-management pension plan trust. It can be used where a local union sues its parent international union for breach of the international's constitution.

If the contract has a clause stating that the union will not strike during the agreement, a court may issue an injunction against a threatened strike by the union.

Federal and some state laws require the payment of at least time and one-half for each hour worked over 40 hours in a week. Some laws, such as in construction and for government suppliers, also require payment of an overtime rate for hours worked over eight per day. Apparently none of the laws require that paid non-worked time, such as for holidays, vacations, or sick leave be considered as time "worked." However, many union contracts require payment of time and one-half for all hours *paid* (not only hours *worked*) over 40 hours per week.

Sometimes overtime is unavoidable, particularly if there is an emergency. In an emergency the employer is normally permitted to request that any employees who can perform the necessary work be required to work regardless of how many hours overtime are involved so long as the employee's health is not impaired by excessive work.

Sometimes overtime is separated into shift or scheduled overtime and unscheduled overtime. Shift overtime is where all employees on a particular shift are expected to work overtime, either before or after the hours for their regular shift, or an extra day, such as Saturday. Many contracts provide that if the employer gives a

Overtime

stated amount of notice, such as 24 hours, of the
overtime, that an employee who fails or refuses
to work the scheduled overtime may be disciplined, unless he has an excuse acceptable to
the employer for not being available. Some contracts permit an employee to reject the working
of some scheduled overtime, after giving a required prior notice.

Unscheduled overtime is often required due
to what the employer considers to be an emergency. Some employees, such as in maintenance,
or in law enforcement or firefighting, are informed before being hired that the nature of
their work requires the availability to work overtime. Unions in contracts usually recognize the
necessity for unscheduled overtime, but negotiate a minimum number of hours' payment,
such as two hours for each "call out" from home,
and a special "premium" or "penalty" rate, such
as time and one-half or double time for unscheduled overtime.

Some employers assign a particular employee
or group of employees to be on "standby" nights
or weekends, and all emergency calls will be
directed to them. Some employers provide employees on standby with a "page boy" or similar
radio buzzer, or pay employees standby pay, or
both.

**Union
negotiation
procedure**
There comes a point in many labor negotiations when the employer and the union are unable to agree upon what the other side is asking
for, or are unwilling to drop a proposal. This is
called an impasse. When the union and the employer are at an impasse, they may have no

obligation to meet with the other party in further meetings unless one side indicates that it has changed its position.

One common method to attempt to reach an agreement is for either side to request the services of a government mediator. The Federal Mediation and Conciliation Service provides government mediators in various cities throughout the country. Many states also have one or more labor mediators. A mediator does not have authority to tell the union or the employer what they shall agree to. He can only make recommendations. His main job is to attempt to get the parties to reach an agreement. He is not particularly concerned about the terms of that agreement, or whether it is "fair"—only that the parties reach an agreement.

If you sit in on labor negotiations representing a union, you will want to follow the advice of the chairman of your negotiating committee. The employer has a chairman or spokesman for its negotiating committee. The chairman is the main speaker for that side and it is usually he who states any change in position. If you are chosen as a member of a negotiation committee, you will not be expected to participate in the negotiations unless your chairman okays it in advance or unless he gives you some kind of signal that it is okay for you to speak up or answer. Negotiators vary considerably in their technique and you will soon learn how your spokesman wants you to conduct yourself in negotiations.

Any negotiator can ask for a caucus of its side

in negotiation. This is not considered to be a sign or evidence of a weakness in one's position. From time to time, in a labor negotiation meeting a member of a negotiating committee may want to discuss their position or some proposal or probable position of the other side with other members of the committee.

If a union is not satisfied with the employer's position in negotiations, and after a mediator is called in, the union may decide to hold a meeting of the employees and to conduct a vote to determine whether the employees should authorize the union to strike. The constitution and by-laws of many unions require a vote by the membership before a valid strike can be conducted. In general there is no legal requirement as to who should be permitted to vote on the question whether there is a strike. This varies from union to union. Sometimes the ballot is worded so that if an employer's offer is rejected the employees at the same time authorize the union's officials to call a strike whenever they want to. Many unions permit only members in good standing to vote on whether the employees should go on strike. Some unions permit any member in good standing to vote on whether to strike, whether or not those members are working for an employer directly involved in those negotiations. For example, if a local union represents employees of ten plants and there is a vote to see whether the employees at your plant go on strike, some unions permit a member of the union employed at another plant to vote. Many unions permit only union members to vote, not others, even if they are employed at the plant which may be struck. A common exception is that when a union is negotiating for a first contract, it may not have many employees signed up as members and it may permit all employees at that plant to vote on whether to strike.

The constitution of many international or national unions provides for the payment of strike benefits for a strike that is authorized by following procedures set out in the constitution. If those procedures are not followed, the strike is probably not properly authorized and the national or international will not pay the strike benefits.

Many unions, prior to a strike, will present the union's position as to why it believes a strike is necessary at a meeting of the central labor council, which usually consists of representatives of most of the unions in a particular city. If the central labor council authorizes or ratifies the strike, it will then urge other unions and their members to support the strike. This means that members of other unions will be expected to refuse to cross the picket lines, and if those members do, they may be subject to a fine by their own union. In some instances an employer may "permanently replace" his employees who refuse to cross a picket line at another employer's plant; if the contract has a "no strike clause" the employer may fire employees who refuse to cross a picket line at another employer's plant.

In the construction industry, the various craft unions in a city often form a building trades council. The building trades council holds regular meetings and votes on whether to support or ratify a proposed strike of any particular union, usually a union in the building and construction industry. One common function of building trades councils is to determine the procedure to be used in "informational" or "union standards" picketing of a non-union contractor or contractors working in the area.

If an employer and a union are unable to reach an agreement in negotiations and a strike is called, pickets are usually posted to advise employees, the public, and other unions of the labor dispute. Many unions require that employees on strike take turns doing picket duty for a few hours. A well organized union usually gives to pickets printed instructions about what to do and what not to do when acting as a picket for the union. If pickets engage in acts of violence against individuals who work during the strike or who attempt to cross the picket line, the pickets and union officers may be guilty of a crime, and they, together with the union, may be liable for money damages. The union may be found to have committed an unfair labor practice and a court may grant an injunction against the violence.

Employees have a legal right to work during a strike even though their union calls a strike. The National Labor Relations Act permits employees to strike or not to strike, as each individual chooses. In most strikes the union attempts to shut down completely the operations of the employer involved in the strike. Some employers, however, attempt to continue to do business as usual during a strike. Employers may hire employees during the strike. If these new hires are told that they will become regular employees even when the strike ends, then those employees are "permanent replacements" for employees out on strike. When a permanent replacement is hired an employee out on strike has, in effect lost his job. However, when the strike finally ends each striker may inform the employer, either directly or through his union, that he is interested in returning to work in his old or a similar job. In this situation, even if the employee has been permanently replaced, the employer must keep his name on a preferential hiring list, and if there is a vacancy in a job that he can do, he must be given first choice at that job, before hiring an outside or new employee. The employer can require that employees wanting to return to work after a strike notify him regularly, such as once a month in writing, or he will automatically take the striker's name off of the preferential hiring list.

The law is not always clear as to under what circumstances employees retain, or continue to earn, benefits while they are on strike. As a general rule, if an employee is not permanently replaced, he continues to earn seniority during the term of the strike. However, if certain benefits, such as paid vacations, paid sick leave, etc., are earned only for so many days paid or for so many days worked, rather than for so many days with an employer, then an employee does not earn those benefits while he is on strike.

An employee may be entitled to vacation pay when he goes on strike, unless his employer has agreed to pay vacation pay only at a particular time, such as the date shown on approved vacation schedules. If an employer pays for fringe benefit plans such as hospital insurance, pension plan, dental care, etc. if an employee *works* so many hours or is *paid* so many hours a month, then the employer will not usually make these payments for an employee while he is out on strike. An employee should contact his union to determine whether he can make these payments direct to the insurance carrier or trustee, in order to avoid losing these benefits.

If an employee in the bargaining unit on strike has a good reason to go into the plant while it is being picketed and does not want to be subject to a fine by his union, he may ask the picket captain or other union agent for a pass to go into the plant, telling the picket captain he needs to go in. If the picket captain finds that the employee is going into the plant to get some personal possessions, such as his personal tools or equipment or to perform only emergency work for the employer, the picket captain will probably give the employee such a pass. However, if the picket captain learns that the employee will probably be doing work which is normally done by people out on strike and that work is not an emergency, he will probably deny the pass. A threat of a fine made to someone not in the bargaining unit on strike may be an unlawful threat.

An employer may lockout employees before or during a strike. For example, if a union and an employer in negotiations are at or near an impasse and the employer believes that it had rather "bring to a head" a smoldering labor dispute now rather than at a later time, such as during his annual peak season of work, then the employer may tell employees that they cannot come to work. An employer may continue to do business during a lockout by using supervisors, friends, and employees hired temporarily—only for the duration of the strike. When the strike ends he must provide regular employment to those employees who were locked out, even if he has to terminate or layoff all of the temporary replacements hired during the strike. (Compare this with a strike when the employer may operate with permanent or temporary replacements.)

Lockouts

When a strike or lockout is settled the employer and the union often agree in writing as to the status of employees. Some strike or lockout settlements provide that strikers will be returned to work, unless they have an equal job elsewhere or if they fail to report to work by a given date. After a strike the employer's volume of business is often down and he is unable or unwilling to return to work all of the strikers immediately. Sometimes a schedule is worked out in a strike settlement agreement, with a stated number of employees returning to work each week for several weeks, or as the production or other demands of the business require it.

Settlements

Union fines for working during a strike

If an employee who is a member of the union wants to exercise his right to work during a strike or picketing, he could be subject to a fine from his union. If he wants to work but to avoid a fine he could resign or terminate his membership in the union. Unless the constitution or by-laws of the union state a detailed procedure as to how to resign or terminate, the usual method is for the member to send a letter to the union, keeping a copy for himself, clearly stating his intent. For example, a member could send a letter such as the following:

I hereby apply for a withdrawal card from the _____ union, Local _____, effective imme-diately. If this request for a withdrawal card is not granted I hereby give notice to terminate my membership in the union, effective immediately. Signed, _____, Book Number _____.

If a union fines a member for working during a strike it may be a lawful fine, particularly if he is a "voluntary" or "full" member of the union. If an employee joined the union only be-cause he was required to do so to keep his job under the union security clause in the contract with the employer, he may not be subject to valid discipline by the union. The decisions dif-fer on this issue. If an employee believes that he was improperly fined by a union, he should insist upon a written statement as to what it is alleged that he did, which members or officers of the union filed charges against him, and which section or sections of the union's constitution and bylaws were allegedly violated. The employee should then insist upon a hearing before the union's trial board, often consisting of its executive board. This meeting will probably be scheduled an evening at the union hall some weeks in the future. The employee should be prepared to present his side of the story, after having analyzed the sections of the constitution and bylaws involved, and to have any witnesses who will speak in his favor. If the employee has any documents which help prove his point bring them also, with duplicate photocopies. The employee should have an outline of his testimony with names and dates. Many union executive boards try to give a member a fair trial and the employee may convince them that he did not act improperly. If however, the trial board of the union finds that an employee-member violated the constitution and bylaws, and orders some disciplinary action to be taken against him, such as a fine or the cancellation of union membership, he may then decide to appeal to the national or international union. The union's constitution probably outlines the appeal procedure to be followed. Federal law requires that if a union has a disciplinary procedure that members be informed of that procedure—see pages 163 and 164.

If a member's appeal was not granted, or after a period of time, usually four months from the date that the charges were brought against him, the member may sue the union. The member may hire an attorney to file a complaint in federal court under Title I, the "Bill of Rights" part of the Labor Management Reporting and

Disclosure Act of 1959. The court may order that the charges against the member be stricken, that his membership be reinstated in good standing, that the union remove from its records any evidence that he allegedly violated the constitution and bylaws because of that incident, and it may grant money damages to the member. On the other hand, the court may decide that the union did not act improperly by disciplining the member.

Duties of unions

A union that is certified by the NLRB, or that is under the Railway Labor Act, or is otherwise recognized by an employer as the exclusive bargaining representative for a particular group of employees, has acquired certain legal rights to be their "exclusive" bargaining representative. The union also has certain obligations and duties toward those employees, even though they are not a member of the union.

The union which represents a group of employees cannot engage in "hostile or invidious discrimination" against any individual it represents. For example, a union cannot refuse to process an employee's grievance because he is a member of a minority group or because he has filed and pressed charges at some time in the past against officers of the union. If the union that represents an employee has failed to represent him fairly, the employee may go to the NLRB to file an unfair labor practice charge against the union.

A union has almost the same duties as has an employer to avoid discrimination against an individual under the antidiscrimination laws of the federal government and of various states. For example, if a union fails to represent an employee fairly because he is a member of a minority group the union may be violating those anti-discrimination laws, thus committing an unfair practice. The union may also be liable for money damages to the employee, particularly if it causes an employer to fail to hire him or to terminate his employment.

part four

If an employee is laid off or terminated

If an employee is laid off or terminated— whether or not there is a union

If an employee is laid off or terminated he should go to the state employment office in his city and register for employment and for unemployment insurance payments. The federal government has established a system of unemployment compensation in which all 50 states participate.

Unemployment insurance

The federal government sets minimum standards required for state unemployment insurance plans and reimburses the states for a large portion of the cost of operating the state employment offices and for distributing unemployment insurance benefits. In many states the employer pays the entire premium or cost of unemployment insurance by a percentage tax of its payroll. In some states employees also make a contribution to unemployment insurance by a small deduction from their paychecks each month.

When an individual files a written claim at his state employment office for unemployment compensation a copy of that claim form will be sent to his most recent employer. The employer has a stated number of days to contest the claim by making a written statement as to why he believes the "claimant" is not entitled to benefits. In most cases the employer does not contest the claim and after the waiting period the individual will be paid a weekly benefit check. This waiting period may be only one week if the claimant was laid off, but in many states it is several weeks longer if he voluntarily quit or was terminated for good cause. The state employment office may agree with the employer's report that there is probable cause for denying benefits. The claimant may then in writing request that the employment office schedule a hearing. This will be held within the next few weeks at the local state employment office. The claimant and the employer should each get from the employment office a copy of their rules and regulations and ask them in general about the issues to be discussed in the hearing. Each side should then plan its testimony and determine whether any other witnesses, such as co-workers who knew the reasons for the termination or leaving the job, should be required to testify. Each side may also present copies of any written letters or other documents from the employer to the claimant. Keep a duplicate copy. In the hearing the testimony will be recorded, usually by a tape recorder. The hearing officer acts impartially. The proceding is much less formal than a court trial. A few weeks after the close of the hearing, the hearing officer will usually issue a recommended decision, either recommending that the claimant be granted benefits of a particular amount or that the claim or benefits be denied. The loser, either the claimant or the employer, can appeal, usually to the director of a state employment office. An appeal may then be made to a state trial court. If the employment office or court finds that a claimant is entitled to weekly benefits, the state will begin payments even though the employer appeals the ruling granting benefits.

An individual is not usually eligible for unemployment benefits unless he has been paid a minimum of wages for a minimum number of weeks in his prior "base year." However, some federal laws passed at least on a temporary basis, may provide "extended" benefits for an individual even if he does not have this minimum number of hours of earnings in the previous benefit year. An employee should check with his local employment office to have them help him determine whether he may be eligible for benefits.

The benefits are usually based upon a percentage, such as two thirds, of the average weekly earnings in your state. If a claimant has dependents he may be entitled to additional benefits. A claimant is entitled to benefits only for a stated period of time such as 26 weeks or 52 weeks, depending in part upon how long he was employed. When a claimant exhausts his normal benefits or uses them up he may be entitled to extended benefits provided under special temporary emergency laws.

In many states a claimant must report weekly to the state employment office to pick up a check. Some states mail the unemployment check out. In most states a claimant must be ready, available, and willing to take other work. If a claimant turns down a job with substantially equal pay and conditions as the job he left, his benefits may then be terminated unless he can show that he refused the job for good cause.

Layoff pay

Many employers have a practice of permitting an employee upon layoff to receive pay for all accrued unused vacation. Some employers have an additional severance pay policy, often based upon the number of weeks that an employee was employed. Some unions have negotiated a formal supplemental unemployment benefit plan whereby for each year of employment an employee is entitled to a stated number of weeks of payment of a stated percentage of his normal wages. For example, if an employee was employed by that employer for five years and for the last year his wage rate was $8,000, he may be entitled to 10 weeks of supplemental unemployment benefits which pays 80 percent of his normal wages.

Anti-discrimination laws

If an employee was laid off or terminated because he is a member of a minority group, or because of his race, color, national origin, citizenship, religion, sex, age, or physical handicaps it may be in violation of the federal civil rights act or in violation of state law. However, if an employee does not perform the job needed in a satisfactory manner, his employer may layoff or terminate him even if he is a member of a minority group.

If an employer terminates an individual, male or female, for failure to comply with the employer's rules concerning length of hair or beard the case decisions differ on whether this is an unfair employment practice. If the employer can show a bona fide occupational qualification for his rule, such as in a food processing plant where health or other sanitation requirements prohibit long hair, then the employer may enforce this rule. Many courts rule that if an individual frequently deals with the public that the employer can set minimum grooming standards, including the length of hair and beard.

Some courts have held that if an employer has the same policy concerning length of hair for males and females that the various civil rights laws are not applicable. Courts have ruled that to prohibit long hair does not discriminate on the basis of sex, since either males or females can have long hair. Courts have also ruled that to prohibit long hair or a beard does not discriminate on the basis of race, since members of almost any race may have a long hair or beard.

If an employee has unusual religious observances, such as the refusal to work on Saturday or after sundown on Friday, and celebrates a day of rest on other than a Sunday, an employer may be required to make "reasonable accomodations" to his religious beliefs. However, if an employer upon hiring informed an employee that he must be ready to be available to work overtime evenings or Saturdays, and he did not express an objection to these hours at that time, then the employer may properly later discipline the employee, including layoff or termination, if he fails to work those hours as needed by the employer's operation of business.

If an employee is physically or mentally handicapped he may be protected by the anti-discrimination laws, provided that he has the necessary skills to perform particular work. If, due to cutback in production or the rearrangement of jobs for business reasons, the employer finds it impractical to continue to pay employees who can only perform a limited number of jobs no longer needed, then the employer may layoff or terminate employees with the ability to do only a particular job that is no longer needed.

Discrimination versus seniority

Many employers, particularly those who do business with the federal government, either as suppliers or in the construction industry, may have signed an "affirmative action plan" in which the employer agrees to hire a stated number of members of various minority groups by various "target dates." If an employer has such an affirmative action plan and he has hired in the last few years a considerable number of minority group employees and there is a subsequent layoff of employees, whom should he layoff? Common industry practice is to layoff employees with the least amount of seniority, provided that the senior employees can do the work needed. This practice often adversely affects members of minority groups who have recently been employed. The federal Equal Employment Opportunity Commission may rule that if a seniority plan used in determining who is laid off has an adverse effect upon recently hired members of minority groups or members of a particular sex, the seniority layoff plan may be invalid. Some courts have ruled that the "quotas" of minority groups, required by affirmative action plans, applies only to the hiring of minorities, but does not protect minorities against layoffs. There will be many court decisions in the next few years over this issue, since many union contracts provide for the layoff first of employees with the least seniority. If a member of a minority group or of a particular sex is laid off as a result of not having enough seniority, he may contact his state unfair employment practices agency if his state has such an agency; if not he may contact the federal Equal Employment Opportunities Commission at its regional office. See Appendix C for a list of those offices. Those agencies can advise an individual whether his layoff may be an unfair practice which would justify the filing of a complaint against an employer, a union, or both.

If an employee is laid off or terminated—where a union represents him

If there is a union contract in effect and an employee is laid off or terminated he should read the sections of the contract dealing with layoff or termination. A layoff is a separation, usually "involuntary," from employment due to lack of work. A termination is a permanent release from employment, with or without just cause. Many contracts provide that the employer may lay off or terminate "probationary" or new employees without just cause. Contracts often also permit the termination or layoff of "casual," temporary, or seasonal employees without just cause.

Types of seniority

Many contracts provide that after the completion of a probationary period of a stated length, such as three months, that an employee becomes a "regular" employee, and he will be given credit for seniority since the date of hire. Some employers have several types of seniority. "Company seniority" is earned by having been employed by that employer without a "break in service" due to quitting, termination, or other stated reasons, such as a long layoff. Many employers also have separate seniority at the particular plant, store, or other business location ("plant or store seniority"). Contracts often provide for a further breakdown of seniority by a major department of the employer ("departmental seniority"). In addition, in each work group there often is an additional kind of seniority, usually used in determining when employees in that work group take their vacation period or who gets preference in shifts to work or days off ("work group seniority").

Employees who are laid off are usually entitled to be recalled if the employer's business later picks up and he can use their skills. However, after a long layoff employees may "lose

their seniority" and lose their right to be recalled. If the employer has no clear policy as to
when this "cutoff date" for loss of seniority occurs, then employees on layoff may retain their
right to be recalled for several years, if they
keep the employer informed of their current
address. Some contracts are interpreted to provide that if an employee is laid off and he gets
an equal job elsewhere, which is considered by
the new employer to be a "permanent" job, then
the employee may not have the right to be recalled. Employees who have been terminated
rather than laid off usually have no right to be
recalled or reemployed.

Some contracts permit employees to "share
the work" in case of a cutback in production, so
that employees with less seniority are not laid
off. Some contracts prohibit the working of overtime if employees are on layoff. However, most
employers object to this—the particular department that works overtime may not be able to use
the skills of employees who are on layoff, due
to their lack of training or experience. Most
unions and many employees object to a requirement that all employees cut back their hours
rather than have a layoff, since the employees
with seniority are thus required to suffer along
with the newer employees. If employees are laid
off they are usually entitled to unemployment
compensation benefits while those who continue
to work are enjoying the benefits acquired by
seniority, namely full-time employment. If employees work a "short" work week none may be
eligible for unemployment compensation.

Where company-wide seniority, rather than only departmental seniority is used for layoffs, all employees may be subject to layoff, even though only one department has little work. For example, if a company has three departments and only department "C" is slow, where there is company wide seniority then those employees in department "C" who have particular skills and company seniority may retain their employment but employees in departments "A" or "B" who have little skills or length of service may be laid off. If, on the other hand, that employer uses departmental seniority for layoffs and recalls, then all employees in department "C" would probably be laid off, regardless of how long they have been with the employer, while newer or less skilled employees in departments "A" and "B" would keep their jobs.

If women or blacks, for example, have been discriminated against in the past by placing them in departments with lower-paying jobs, then the federal or state antidiscrimination laws may prohibit layoffs by department.

Some contracts are interpreted to provide that if there is a cutback in production, an employee with seniority may have a chance to "bump" into another job even though he has not done that job before. He may have a right to an opportunity of a stated number of days of learning on the new job to determine whether he can do it. While he is learning to do the job, the employee who has done it may either be laid off, or in turn may "bump" into a still-lower classified job. Employers often object to any proposed contract that would require bumping, since considerable time is involved in training several employees to do a new job. Some union contracts compromise by listing jobs considered to be skilled and providing that employees cannot bump into those skilled jobs unless they have had experience in those jobs.

If an employer buys or is bought by a different employer, and if there is a merger or consolidation of the operations of two or more employers, then problems of seniority and layoff are important. One common method used in determining seniority when two or more operations are merged into one operation is to combine seniority by giving full credit for past company or departmental seniority for employment in each prior company or plant. This is called dovetailing of seniority. There are various other forms of this seniority. One common method, alternate layoffs, provides, for example, that if a plant with 300 employees is merged into a plant with 100 employees and there should later be a layoff in the new plant having 400 employees, that 3 employees from the larger plant would be laid off for each employee who had worked in the smaller plant.

Regardless of whether the same union represents employees at both operations that have been consolidated or otherwise merged, it has a high degree of responsibility to employees in both operations to treat them fairly. For example, if the employees at the employer's operation "A" were represented by union "A" and employees at another operation "B" which is

Mergers or consolidations of employers

merged into operation "A" were either non-union or were represented by a different union then union "A" has a high degree of responsibility to be fair to both groups of employees. If, in this example, if union "A" claims that employees of the old plant that disappeared by merger have lost all their seniority and employment benefits, and must start as new employees, then those employees may have certain rights of action against union "A." If union "A" refuses to accept past service credit for employees at the old plant because they were not members of that union, the union may then have committed an unfair labor practice. Any employees of the former plant or their union may file an unfair labor practice charge against union "A." The National Labor Relations Board will then conduct an investigation and may order the hiring of those employees at the new plant, with back pay from union "A," or so order the employer also if the employer agrees with union "A." Former employees of plant "B" could also sue union "A" in federal court, claiming "hostile or invidious discrimination" against them.

Obviously, in a situation like the above example, a union or an employer should seek legal advice before commitments are made. If there is some doubt as to whether particular employees should be represented by a union, or by which of two competing unions, the employer or a union should consider filing a petition for an election with the NLRB.

If an employee is laid off, terminated, or discharged and the union contract covering him has a provision for the filing of a grievance, then he may be required to file a grievance before the NLRB or a court will help him. If the union contract provides for the arbitration of such a layoff or termination, then a laid-off employee will ordinarily be required to take his grievance to arbitration if it is not settled to his satisfaction. If a grievance can be taken to arbitration neither the employees nor the union can picket, strike, or successfully sue directly in court, alleging that the layoff or termination was in violation of the contract. One exception is that if an employee can show that his layoff or termination was because of his race, color, national origin, sex, or age, he may then file a complaint with the federal Equal Employment Opportunity Commission or his state anti-discrimination commission (if the state has such a law and agency), or he may sue directly in court, claiming such discrimination.

Union agents have some discretion to refuse to spend the union's funds to take a grievance to an arbitrator, if the union in good faith believes that it has little chance of persuading an arbitrator that the employer's action was in violation of the contract. If a union that represents an employee flatly refuses to take his grievance to arbitration (and the contract provides for arbitration) then he can probably sue the union in court or file with the NLRB unfair labor practice charges against the union. However, the employee will not win if the union can show that it used "good faith" in its belief that it could not win the arbitration case. The em-

Discrimination by unions

ployee will probably win in court if he can show that the union did not in "good faith" decide that there was little chance of winning an arbitration, or if the union discriminated against him because of his race, color, national origin, or sex in refusing to process the grievance to arbitration.

In a union attempts to cause an employer to discharge an employee because he is not a member in good standing, this attempt by the union may be lawful if there is a contract with a lawful "union security" provision between that union and the employer and that employee has not complied with the union security provision. For example, if the union contract requires "membership in good standing" in the union after 30 days of employment and the employee has not offered to pay to the union its regular initiation fee and the first month's periodic dues, then the union's attempt to have him terminated is probably lawful (except in a state with a "right to work" law). But if the union insists upon "full membership" or the payment of a union fine or assessment, rather than only the payment of the initiation fee and first month's dues, then the union has probably acted unlawfully. If an employee believes that the union's attempt to have the employer fire him for not having complied with the contract's union security clause is improper, the employee should notify his employer in detail as to why he believes that he has complied with the "union security clause." The employer then has a duty to make a further investigation to see if the employee's version is correct, and if he finds that it is correct he should refuse to terminate the employee. If the union is successful in its unlawful attempt to have an employee terminated, he may file unfair labor practice charges with the NLRB against either the union or the employer, or both. The NLRB will investigate the charge, and if it finds that there is cause to believe that the law has been violated, it will eventually order the employee reinstated, and will order the union or the employer, or both, to pay full back wages.

part five

Summary of federal and state labor and employment agencies and laws

NLRB and unfair labor practices

An employee may file a charge with the NLRB against either an employer or a union, claiming that it engaged in an unfair labor practice. There is a six month "statute of limitations" in the law, so that a charge may not be filed based upon an event that occurred more than six months earlier. The NLRB regional office will provide forms and help in preparing that form if requested. The "charge" form must be signed before it is filed. The NLRB will mail a copy to the employer and to the union. There is no fee by the NLRB to file a charge, even though it results in a lengthy trial and appeals. A "charging party" is not required to be represented by an attorney, but he may hire one and pay his usual fee. The charging party's attorney will assist the NLRB's attorney.

Charge form

Rights of employees

The heart of the National Labor Relations Act is Section 7, which states the rights of employees. Certain acts of an employer infringe upon those rights and constitute an employer unfair labor practice. Certain acts of a union or its agents infringe upon those rights of employees and constitute a union unfair labor practice. However, there are many possible acts of an employer or a union that are unfair, yet do not constitute an unfair labor practice. Section 7 states as follows:

> Employees shall have the right to self-organization, to form, join, or assist labor organizations, to bargain collectively through representatives of their own choosing, and to engage in other concerted activities for the purpose of collective bargaining or other mutual aid or protection, and shall also have the right to refrain from any or all of such activities except to the extent that such right may be affected by an agreement requiring membership in a labor organization as a condition of employment at authorized in Section 8(a)(3).

Employer unfair labor practices

Interference, restraint, or coercion

Section 8(a)(1) makes it an unfair labor practice for an employer "to interfere with, restrain, or coerce employees in the exercise of rights guaranteed in Section 7."

If the employer has committed any unfair labor practice it automatically violates Section 8(a)(1). Other types of employer activity which would be an "independent" violation of Section 8(a)(1) are:

1. Questioning employees about their union activities or membership in circumstances

that will tend to create fear by the employees;

2. Spying on union meetings;
3. Threatening employees with loss of jobs or
   benefits if they should join or vote for a
   union;
4. Granting wage increases timed to discour-
   age employees from forming or voting for
   a union; or
5. Disciplining a group of employees for
   peacefully complaining about wages or
   working conditions even though there is no
   union involved.

Section 8(a)(2) makes it an unfair labor
practice for an employer "to dominate or interfere with the formation or administration" of a
union "or contribute financial or other support
to it." An employer violates this section by:

Unlawful assistance to union

1. Taking an active part in organizing a committee or plan to represent employees in
   dealing with the employer regarding wages
   or working conditions;
2. Bringing pressure on employees to join a
   union except in the enforcement of a lawful
   union security agreement;
3. Permitting one of two or more unions which
   are competing to represent employees to
   solicit employees on company property during working hours but denying that privi-
   lege to other unions;
4. Recognizing, negotiating, or signing a contract with a union that does not represent a
   majority of his employees (except that in

the construction industry it may not be unlawful) ; or

5. When buying an additional plant or store
   or similar business to agree to put those
   employees under an existing contract without proof that the union represents a majority of those employees.

Discrimination   Section 8(a)(3) makes it unlawful for an
employer to refuse to hire, or to discharge or
otherwise discriminate in employment terms or
conditions against an employee because he is a
member of a union. An employer cannot:

Fire an employee because he engaged in a
lawful strike.

Close or sell a plant or a department because
the employees there are organizing or have
organized a union with which the employer
does not want to deal.

Refuse to hire an employee because he is or
is not a member of a particular union.

Fire an employee because he is not a member
of the union when he has not been employed for 30 days (7 days in the construction industry).

Subcontract out work because a union orga-
nizes the employees in that department.

An employer cannot fire employees who engage in a lawful strike, but he may "permanently replace" them. However, if the striker
asks to return and the employer later has a job
vacancy the striker can satisfactorily fill, the

employer must then give preference to the striker over a new job applicant.

An employer may terminate employees under the following circumstances: those who strike over a grievance when there is a contract with a "no strike" clause, or which provides for arbitration of that grievance; those who strike in furtherance of an unfair labor practice by a union; those who strike before the union gives to the employer and to a government mediator certain notices near the end of a contract; or those who commit acts of violence during an otherwise lawful strike.

An employer may lay off or terminate for cause an employee even though he is a member of a union.

An employer may not terminate an employee because he is not a member of a union unless there is a contract with a lawful union security provision, the union requests the termination, and the employer believes that the reason for the union's request is that the employee has not offered to pay to the union the uniformly required initiation fee and the regular periodic dues. In a state with a "right to work law" the union cannot require that the employer fire any employee for failure to pay any fee to the union.

Section 8(a)(4) protects an employee who files an election petition or an unfair labor practice charge, or who testifies in an election or unfair labor practice matter before the NLRB. An employer may not refuse to promote, nor may an employer lay off or discharge or otherwise

Protection of witnesses

discipline an employee for using the processes of the NLRB during non-working time.

Refusal to bargain

Section 8(a)(5) requires that an employer bargain in good faith with the union that represents a majority of his employees. This duty to bargain applies to the negotiation of changes in an existing contract.

An employer has a duty upon request of the union to meet and confer with the union at reasonable times and places, in an attempt to reach an agreement. However, the employer cannot be compelled by the NLRB to agree to any particular term or condition of employment or wages the employer has not himself agreed to.

Upon request of the union the employer must supply information "relevant and necessary" to allow the union to bargain intelligently and effectively. This information might include a list of the names, job classifications, wage rates, and date of hire or seniority date for all employees in the bargaining unit represented by the union.

If an agreement is reached on all subjects, upon request of the union, the employer must sign the contract that states their agreement.

The employer cannot make changes from existing wages, hours, terms, or conditions of employment without at least notifying the union of that change. However, if the employer in the past has taken particular action, such as subcontracting without notifying the union, then the employer may continue with past practice. Sometimes a union in a contract agrees that an employer may take particular action without consulting or notifying the union. An employer may also make changes in minor matters without consulting the union. An employer may not usually grant a wage increase without first consulting the union, unless the contract permits it or the employer is following his past practice of granting an increase to individual employees. However, if the employer and the union are negotiating for a contract and the employer has made an offer to the union of a stated amount of wage increase and the parties have reached an "impasse" in bargaining so that neither is willing to change its offer or proposal, then the employer may put into effect its last wage offer.

If there is a contract with a provision that disputes may be taken to arbitration, the NLRB may require the union to go to arbitration rather than to the NLRB.

An individual employee has the right to discuss with his foreman, supervisor, or anyone else in management any particular grievance or complaint and to "adjust" that complaint as long as the "adjustment" agreed to is not inconsistent with the terms of the collective bargaining contract. However, if the employee insists that the union agent be present in the discussion between the employee and the employer, the employer should agree. An individual employee may sign an individual contract of employment with the employer but the terms of that individual contract cannot conflict with the terms of a collective bargaining agreement that also covers him. If there is such conflict then the collective bargaining agreement controls.

If an employer buys part or all of the plant

and equipment and maintains substantially the same suppliers and customers, and hires substantially the same employees of a predecessor employer, it may be a "successor employer." A successor employer usually has a duty to recognize and bargain with the union that represented the seller's employees. However, a successor is usually not bound by the seller's collective bargaining agreement.

Sometimes a group of employers bargain as a group with a union and have a practice of agreeing to the same terms and conditions of employment. Those employers sometimes have a formal association. When they reach an agreement with the union on the terms of a contract it usually applies to all of the employers in that unit. Sometimes each employer signs a copy of the same document, or a spokesman for all of the employers in the unit signs. Such a group is called a "multiemployer bargaining unit." An employer may withdraw from such a bargaining unit if he gives clear notice to the union of his withdrawal at a proper time, before negotiations actually begin in that unit. The union may also withdraw from the unit by giving a "timely" notice to all the employers that it will bargain with them on a separate basis.

Union unfair labor practices

Restraint and coercion

Section 8(b)(1)(A) makes it an unfair labor practice for a union to "restrain or coerce" employees in the exercise of the rights guaranteed in Section 7.

A union may adopt internal rules or bylaws governing its members, and enforce those rules or bylaws to a certain extent without violating the National Labor Relations Act. However, if those rules govern the conduct of a union member in his relation with his employer, then the union, by preparing or enforcing those rules, may restrain or coerce employees in violation of Section 8(b)(1)(A). For example, a union may lawfully fine a member for working during a lawful strike or for not attending a regular union meeting. A union may also terminate the membership of, but not fine, a member who files an NLRB petition to decertify the union. If an employee joined the union only because he is covered by a contract with a union security clause (such as a 30-day or 8-day union shop clause), then the union has less freedom to discipline the member.

Members may be required to first follow the procedure provided in the union's constitution and bylaws, such as filing a charge within the union, so long as that procedure does not require more than four months' time, before the NLRB will rule that the union's conduct violated the National Labor Relations Act. However, the statute of limitations for the National Labor Relations Act is only six months, so a charge should be filed with the NLRB within that time period.

If union members send to the union a notice of their resignation, they may then engage in conduct, such as going through a picket line to work, and if the union then attempts to discipline them such as by a fine, the union may violate Section 8(b)(1)(A). The members may not be required to follow the complete procedure provided in the union constitution or bylaws for resigning from union membership if that procedure is too lengthy and members are not clearly informed of the procedure. The member should send a signed letter (keeping a copy for himself) by registered mail or certified mail, return receipt requested, to the union (see page 114). The letter should clearly state that the member is resigning his membership, and it should be signed by the member, stating his address and book or union member number. The union cannot later attempt to get the employer to fire him under the terms of a "union security" agreement, so long as he offers to pay to the union an amount equal to the union's initiation fee and each month's current dues.

A union that is the exclusive bargaining representative of employees owes to them a duty to represent them fairly whether or not they are a member of the union, and regardless of their race, color, or sex.

Other activities by a union or its agent (such as a business agent, and usually a steward or individuals picketing) that violate Section 8(b)(1)(A) include:

1. Mass-picketing that prevents employees or others from going into or out of the employer's premises,
2. Acts of violence on the picket line.

3. Threatening to injure nonstriking employees,

4. Threatening employees that they will lose their job if they are not a member of the union in good standing (but if there is a valid contract in effect with a union shop clause such statement may not be an unlawful threat),

5. Entering into a contract with an employer when the union has not been chosen by a majority of the employees in that bargaining unit,

6. Maintaining a seniority arrangement with an employer that is discriminatory, because it favors union members or individuals of a particular race, color, or sex, and

7. Refusing to register or refer an individual in the union-operated exclusive hiring hall because he is not a member in good standing with the union.

Restraint and coercion of employer representatives

Section 8(b)(1)(B) makes it unlawful for a union "to restrain or coerce an employer in the selection of his representatives for the purposes of collective bargaining or the adjustment of grievances."

A union cannot insist that an employer not have a particular individual, such as a supervisor, labor consultant, or attorney, represent the employer in contract negotiations or in handling grievances. A union cannot threaten to discipline a member because of acts he did for the employer while acting as a supervisor for the employer. A union cannot strike one or more members of a multiemployer association with an object to get them to sign individual contracts and break away from the association.

Discrimination in employment

Section 8(b)(2) makes it an unfair labor practice for a union "to cause or attempt to cause an employer to discriminate against an employee in violation of subsection (a) (3). . . ."

A union violates Section 8(b)(2) by requesting that an employer discharge an employee because he is not a member of that union, or not a member in "good standing" unless there is a lawful "union security" agreement. A "closed shop," requiring that an employee be a member of the union before he can be hired, is made unlawful. Any union security agreement must permit the employee a 30-day "grace period" before he can be required to make any payment to the union. However, in the construction industry he can be required to make such payment after 7 days.

An employee cannot be discharged because he is not a member of the union so long as he has offered to pay any initiation fee uniformly required and the periodic dues, such as monthly dues. This offer should be in the form of cash or money order, although a personal check is usually considered to be sufficient. An employee cannot lawfully be discharged if he offers to pay such initiation fees and the current month's dues plus any other dues that began during the current collective bargaining agreement, or from the period 30 days after the employee was hired

(7 days in construction), whichever is later. An employee cannot be required to sign an application for membership in the union or to take an oath of allegiance to the union or to its constitution and bylaws. An employee also cannot be required to pay a fine or an assessment, so long as he pays or offers to pay the initiation fees uniformly required and the periodic dues. However, the union can attempt to collect a fine or assessment from a member of the union by internal union procedures, and in some states it may then go into court to seek payment of that fine or assessment. The union cannot insist that the employer fire the employee because he has not paid such fine or assessment.

Approximately 20 states have passed a "right to work law." These prohibit agreements between an employer and a union which require payment of dues or fees to a union or membership in a union. The National Labor Relations Act as amended permits these state laws. If an employee who lives in a state with such a "right to work law" chooses not to make any payment of initiation fees or dues to the union, it cannot request that the employer fire the employee, and any provision in a collective bargaining agreement requiring membership or payment of fees to the unions would be invalid and not enforceable. However, an employee may join a union if he wishes.

If an employer and a union have an agreement or practice that if the employer hires anyone he must first give a hiring hall operated by the union the opportunity to refer or dispatch

Hiring halls

any applicant, it is usually lawful unless the dispatcher, in making referrals, favors union members over others. The union may charge referral fees if the amount of the fee is reasonably related to the cost of operating the hiring hall. The union may also give preference to "local people" in referrals, at least in the construction industry. If the dispatcher discriminated in referrals against individuals who are not members in good standing of the local, the union violates this section and is liable for any back pay lost because of this discriminatory practice.

If the dispatcher refuses to let an individual register with an "exclusive" hiring hall, and the individual believes that he is qualified to perform the work, he should inquire about the procedure for testing applicants. If there is an employer–union committee the individual should present evidence of training or experience (such as paycheck stubs, letters from employers, or military officers) to the committee or the dispatcher. Keep a photocopy of any documents provided. Look for any document on the bulletin board stating rules for the hiring hall and the appeal procedure. An individual should follow that appeal procedure if he believes he was wrongfully denied the right to register. If he does not get a satisfactory answer within a few days, the individual should visit, phone, or write the NLRB regional office and ask to file an unfair labor practice charge. A job applicant is not required to first follow any procedures set out in the collective bargaining agreement or in the hiring hall rules before filing a charge of discrimination against the union. However, after filing a charge, the NLRB may require him to follow that procedure.

If the agreement or practice of the employer permits him to hire from other sources without requiring that job applicants be referred to him by the union hiring hall, the union may in referrals give preference to its members.

Section 8(b)(3) makes it unlawful for a union that represents the employees to refuse to bargain collectively in good faith with the employer.

Refusal to bargain

A union cannot strike at the end of a contract or during the "automatic renewal period" unless it first gives to the employer a 60-day notice to negotiate changes required by Section 8(d) of the National Labor Relations Act, a 30-day notice to the Federal Mediation and Conciliation Service, and a 30-day notice to a state mediator (if that state has a state mediator). The union must also give the other notices (usually 60 to 90 days) required in the collective bargaining agreement. The union must wait until the end of all those time periods before striking. Any employee who strikes before the end of that "cooling-off period" may be fired by the employer. A union must give a hospital a 90 day notice, and a 60 day notice to mediation agencies. If a union plans to strike or picket a hospital it must give an additional 10 day notice to the hospital.

A union that is the exclusive representative of employees has a duty to meet at reasonable times with the employer or his representative and confer in good faith on wages, hours, or other terms or conditions of employment, and if an agreement is reached in negotiations the union must upon request sign a copy of that agreement. A union does not bargain in good faith if it insists that the employer sign its "standard" or "pattern" contract, without concessions or modifications.

The union has a duty to represent fairly all of the employees in the bargaining unit whether they are members of the union or not. A union cannot discriminate against those employees for irrelevant or arbitrary reasons, such as to discriminate against a group of employees because of their race, color, or sex.

Neither a union nor an employer can insist upon "nonmandatory" subjects of bargaining in negotiations. For example, the union cannot insist that the contract cover employees who are outside the bargaining unit certified by the NLRB. It cannot strike or harass an employer, who is a member of a multiemployer bargaining unit, to force that employer to sign a separate contract with the union or to withdraw from the multiemployer unit. The union cannot in negotiations insist that the employer settle a pending grievance other than by taking it to arbitration. The union cannot insist upon an unlawful cause, such as a "hot cargo" agreement or a "closed shop" agreement, or any other form of union security unlawful in that state. The union cannot insist that supervisors who handle grievances for the employer become union members.

Hot cargo

Section 8(e) of the National Labor Relations Act makes it unlawful for an employer or a union to enter into a "hot cargo" agreement. This is an agreement, written or verbal, in which the employer stops or agrees to stop doing business with another employer. In the construction industry such a "hot cargo" agreement is lawful when limited to the contracting or subcontracting of work to be done at the job site, and the union can enforce it by arbitration or a court action but cannot picket or threaten to picket to enforce it. In the garment industry a "hot cargo" agreement may not be unlawful.

Section 8(b)(4)(A) makes it unlawful for a union to request or "induce or encourage" an individual employee not to work, not to handle goods, or to "threaten, coerce, or restrain" an employer or other "person" to force any employer or independent contractor to enter into a "hot cargo" agreement.

Section 8(b)(4)(A) also prohibits such conduct by a union to force or require any employer or independent contractor to join any union, or to join any employer organization.

Forcing independent contractors

It is often difficult to determine whether an individual is an independent contractor or is an employee. In general, if an individual furnishes his own expensive machinery such as a truck or a tractor, if he has considerable right to determine his hours and days of work and the details as to how he does that work, if he does similar work for other employers, and advertises his business, then he is probably an independent contractor, not an employee.

Section 8(b)(4)(B) makes it unlawful for a union to "induce or encourage" an individual not to work or not to handle goods, or to "threaten, coerce, or restrain" an employer or other "person," where the object is to cause that

Secondary boycotts

person not to use or handle the products of anyone else or to stop doing business with him. This
section also prohibits similar conduct where the
object is to require any other employer to bargain with or sign a contract with a union, unless
that union has been certified by the NLRB as the
representative of those employees.

In general, if a union has a labor dispute with
one person or employer (the "primary employer"), it must take steps to limit the effect of
its action against that "primary" on neutrals or
"secondary employers." For example, if a union
has a dispute with a subcontractor who is working at a jobsite where a general contractor and
other persons are employed, the union may picket
the subcontractor with whom it has the dispute
at that jobsite provided that (1) the picket signs
make it clear that the only dispute is with the
subcontractor and not with any other person,
(2) its picketing is limited to times when the
subcontractor's employees are present at the site,
(3) its picketing is limited to places close to the
operation of the subcontractor's employees, and
(4) the subcontractor's employees are engaged
in his normal subcontracting work at those
premises. If a separate gate is established only
for that subcontractor and his employees or deliveries, then the union can picket only at that
gate and not at gates used by others.

It may not be unlawful for a union to picket
or threaten to picket another employer who is an
"ally" of the primary employer. If the primary
and secondary employers are commonly owned
and controlled or have "closely integrated opera-

tions" they may be allies. Likewise, if the secondary employer does "struck work" that would normally be done by the primary, they may be allies.

Section 8(b)(4)(C) makes it unlawful for a union to induce or encourage an individual employee not to work or not to handle goods, or to threaten, coerce, or restrain an employer or other person, where the union has an object to force or require any employer to bargain with or sign a contract with any union. However, if that union has been certified by the NLRB as the bargaining representative, it may be lawful.

Coercion to force recognition

Section 8(b)(4)(D) makes it unlawful for a union to induce or encourage an individual employee not to work or not to handle goods, or to threaten, coerce, or restrain an employer or person, with an object to force or require any employer to assign particular work to a group of employees. However, if that employer is failing to conform to an order of the NLRB or certification of the NLRB, it is not unlawful. For example, if a union representing ironworkers threatens to picket if it is not assigned the work of installing metal roofing then the ironworkers' union may violate this section of the law. However, if the ironworkers' union had won an NLRB election among employees of that employer, or if the NLRB had issued an order awarding this kind of work done by that employer to employees represented by the ironworkers' union, then such threat may not be unlawful.

Jurisdictional disputes

Section 10(k) of the law provides that if

there is such a threat of a work stoppage by a union seeking particular work then the NLRB may schedule a hearing, and upon the basis of evidence presented, the NLRB will make an assignment of the work in dispute to a particular "trade, craft, or class." In the hearing the NLRB will want testimony and documents showing the skills and work involved; any certifications of the union(s) by the NLRB and the past practice by the employer and in the industry; any agreement between union(s) and between the employers and the union; awards of arbitrators, joint boards, or parent unions in the same or related cases; the assignment of work made by the employer; and the efficient operation of the employer's business.

Excessive or discriminatory membership fees

Section 8(b)(5) makes it unlawful for a union that has a "union security agreement" with an employer to charge a fee "which the Board finds excessive or discriminatory under the circumstances." If the employer, for example, has a collective bargaining agreement with a union that provides that after 30 days employees must become a member of the union, then it is unlawful for the union to charge an excessive initiation fee or dues.

The practices and customs of other labor organizations in that industry and the wages paid to the employees will be considered in determining whether the fees are excessive. If a fee is imposed not to provide needed additional revenues for the local union but to maintain in effect a closed shop by a fee so high that it discourages entrance into the industry, then it violates this section. A reinstatement fee for old members slightly higher than the initiation fee for new members may be lawful under this section.

Section 8(b)(6) makes it unlawful for a union "to cause or attempt to cause an employer to pay or deliver or agree to pay or deliver any money or other thing of value in the nature of exaction, for services which are not performed or not to be performed." This section does not prohibit payments such as employees' wages during lunch, rest, waiting, or vacation periods, or for reporting for duty to determine whether work is to be done.

Featherbedding

Section 8(b)(7) makes it unlawful for a union, unless it is "currently certified" as the representative of the employees, to picket or threaten to picket an employer to force the employer to bargain with the union or to sign a contract with it where (*a*) the employer has lawfully recognized a different union, or (*b*) within the last 12 months a "valid" election has been conducted by the NLRB and the union did not win, or (*c*) the picketing continues for more than a reasonable period of time, not more than 30 days, without the filing of a petition for an election.

Picketing for organization, recognition, or bargaining

Sometimes a union claims that its picketing is only to inform the public that the employer does not employ members of the union or have a contract with it. This picketing may be lawful unless "an effect" of the picketing is to induce individuals not to perform services or to make deliveries or pick up goods.

Unions sometimes claim that their picketing is

only to inform the public that the employer does not pay "standard" wages or other benefits. This picketing may be lawful unless it is shown that an object of the picketing is to get employees to join the union or to cause the employer to bargain with or sign a contract with the union.

If a charge is filed claiming that picketing is in violation of Section 8(b)(7)(C), then the employer or an individual (such as an employee) may file a petition for an "expedited" election. If the NLRB regional director finds that the picketing apparently has such a purpose, he may order the election.

Injunctions

If the regional director of the NLRB believes that there is merit to a charge that the union violated Section 8(b)(4) or Section 8(b)(7) and there is current picketing or a work stoppage or the threat of one, he will seek an injunction against the unlawful acts in a federal district court. If the injunction is granted it normally is in effect until the matter is ultimately decided by the Board on its merits.

The regional director may, under another section of the law, seek an injunction against unfair labor practices of either an employer or a union, but this kind of injunction is not common.

Unfair labor practice procedure

If the regional director of the NLRB believes that an employer or a union has committed an unfair labor practice as charged he will first give that party an opportunity to settle the matter. This consists, as a minimum, of the signing of a standard "informal" settlement agreement plus the signing and posting of a "notice" on its bulletin board for at least 60 days. A "formal" settlement agreement consists of a document signed by the parties stating the background facts about the employer or the union, the conduct that is believed to be an unfair labor practice, and an agreement to the entry of an order of the NLRB in a particular form.

If there is no satisfactory signed settlement agreement, the regional director will issue a complaint and schedule a hearing before an NLRB administrative law judge. The charged party (respondent) has at least ten days to file a written answer to the complaint. Failure to answer each claim made in the complaint will be treated as an admission that the claim is true.

The hearing before the judge is usually scheduled about two months after the complaint issues, in the city where the respondent is located or where most of the conduct claimed to be unlawful occurred. The hearing before the judge is formal, similar to a court trial without a jury. The rules of procedure of the federal district courts are followed. A court reporter takes down testimony. The attorney for the NLRB regional director acts as prosecutor, calling witnesses, each of whom is subject to cross-examination. The charging party may also be represented by an attorney, but it is not necessary. since the attorney for the regional director represents the public and the charging party. The respondent is usually represented by an attorney. After the NLRB attorney "closes" his case, the respondent may call witnesses and present testimony. A closing argument may be made and briefs may be filed with the judge.

About two months or more after the trial is completed, the judge prepares a written decision, copies of which are served upon the parties, finding in detail the facts, resolving credibility (deciding who is correct, where there is a dispute as to what happened), and interpreting the law to issue a written decision. Within 20 days, any party may file an appeal (take exceptions) to his decision. The exceptions must state exactly what page and line of the judge's decision is believed to be wrong. A brief, arguing the "facts" and the law from NLRB or court cases, may also be prepared. A copy of the exceptions and brief must be served upon each of the other parties.

A few months later the National Labor Relations Board in Washington, D.C., will issue an order adopting, modifying, or reversing the judge's decision. The decision of the Board may be appealed to a U.S. Circuit Court of Appeals. If the Board finds an unlawful practice and the respondent does not comply with the Board's order, the Board may file a petition for enforcement of its order with the U.S. Circuit Court of Appeals. The decision of the Court may be appealed to the U.S. Supreme Court.

Remedies   The Board's order attempts to remedy any unfair labor practice found. However, the Board does not have authority to punish the respondent, or to force it to admit that it violated the act. The usual language for the Board's notices is "we will not. . . ." The respondent is thus required to agree that it will not engage in certain unlawful acts but it is not required to admit that it has in the past engaged in such acts.

If an employer is found to have unlawfully assisted a union it is required to agree that it will not unlawfully assist the named union. If the employer is found to have unlawfully dominated a union it will be asked to "disestablish" that union. If it is found to have unlawfully discharged an employee because of his union activity, the employer will be asked to reinstate the employee and to pay back pay, plus interest at 6 percent. If the Board finds that an employer has not bargained in good faith with the union it will be asked to sign the notice stating that it will bargain in good faith.

If a union is found to have unlawfully caused the employer to discharge an employee for some reason, other than his failure to pay or offer to pay the uniform initiation fee or periodic dues, then the union will be asked to pay back pay plus interest at 6 percent. The union will also be asked to notify the employer in writing that it has no objections to his taking back the named individual. If the union is found to have charged unlawful fees, such as dues before 30 days of employment, assessments, or excessive or discriminatory fees, then the union will be ordered to refund to employees the unlawful part of any fees paid. If the union is found to have engaged in picketing or other conduct in violation of the law, it will be ordered to "cease and desist" from such unlawful conduct.

Sometimes an unfair labor practice charge is

filed against both an employer and the union and both are found to have committed the unlawful act as charged. The employer and the union are each "jointly and severally" liable. Thus, either the employer or the union could be ordered to pay the complete amount of any money owed.

If the Board finds that the employer unlawfully discharged or refused to take back a striker, the Board may not order that he be paid back pay from the date earlier than the time when he makes an "unconditional" offer to return to work. However, this offer could be made by the union or another employee on that employee's behalf.

If an individual is eligible for back pay because of an unlawful act by an employer or a union or both, he has a duty to look for other similar work in his area. He should register with the state employment office and look for work elsewhere. The Board will deduct earnings from "interim employment" since his discharge, but he may claim credit for expenses of looking for other work. He should keep a record of such expenses. The individual must notify the NLRB agent assigned to the case of his change of address.

Summary of federal and state agencies

The U.S. Department of Labor, headed by the secretary of labor, a member of the president's cabinet, has many activities. They include the following:

1. Administration of the Wage and Hour Law and the Public Contracts Act; the Landrum-Griffin Act as it applies to controls over unions and their relationship with union members; part of the Pension Reform Act of 1974; and the Office of Veterans Reemployment Rights.
2. Coordination of the state-federal public employment offices and unemployment compensation system, apprentice and other training programs.
3. Gathering, analysis, and publication of data about employment, earnings, and cost of living.

This act applies to labor relations between railroads and commercial airlines and unions that represent their employees. It established the National Mediation Board to handle "major disputes" and the Railroad Adjustment Board and airline systems boards to handle "minor disputes," such as arbitration matters.

Railway Labor Act

This independent agency was established under Title VII of the Civil Rights Act of 1964. It is managed by the five-member Equal Employment Opportunity Commission (EEOC). There are regional offices in various cities throughout the country. This act prohibits discrimination in hiring, laying off, promotions, transfers, etc., in employment on the basis of race, color, religion, sex, or national origin. It applies to employers with 15 or more employees, to labor organizations with 15 or more members, and to employment agencies.

Equal Employment Opportunities Commission

Occupational
Safety and
Health Review
Commission

This independent agency was established under the Occupational Safety and Health Act of 1970. The law requires each employer to furnish employment that is free from hazards likely to cause death or serious physical harm to his employees. It provides for establishing safety standards for industry, and for warning labels and posters. An employee or union agent can request that an agent of the Secretary of Labor visit the work area claimed to be unsafe, and if a hazard is found a citation may be issued and a penalty assessed if the hazard is not corrected.

State laws

About 17 states have a State Labor Relations Act that applies to private employers not covered by the federal National Labor Relations Act or the Railway Labor Act. These state acts usually provide for a state agency to conduct elections, and they prohibit certain unfair labor practices of employers, unions, or individuals. Many states also have laws regulating labor relations of county, city, and state governments, public schools and universities, hospitals, and the unions which represent their employees.

Most states have laws requiring the payment of wages when an employee quits or is fired, the payment of an overtime rate under certain conditions, and laws restricting hours and days of work and the type of work which women and minors can do. All states have a law providing a form of insurance for employees injured on the job (workmen's compensation).

Many states have an agency with authority to administer a safety law similar to the federal

Occupational Health and Safety Act. More than half of the states have laws prohibiting discrimination on the basis of race, color, national origin, sex or age.

The Landrum-Griffin Act (Labor-Management Reporting and Disclosure Act of 1959)

This federal law has several requirements to protect the rights of union members. Title I provides a "bill of rights" for union members, but violations of this section can usually be enforced only by the member's hiring a private attorney to sue the union in federal court.

Section 104 of this law gives a union member or any employee covered by a union contract the right to a copy of the contract between the union and his employer.

Title I gives to members the right to nominate and vote on candidates for office in their union, to attend membership meetings and vote on union business, and freedom of speech and assembly. Dues, initiation fees, and assessments can be levied only after a secret ballot vote as provided in that law. A union member cannot be fined, suspended, or otherwise disciplined by the union so long as he pays his dues regularly, unless he is given written charges specifying what he did wrong, a reasonable time to prepare his defense, and a full and fair hearing. If a member believes that his union does not grant him these rights, he should follow the appeal procedure as specified in the constitution and bylaws of the union, but if this appeal procedure requires over four months, he may sue the union in federal court.

Other provisions of the Landrum-Griffin Act require that unions prepare and file with the Department of Labor a detailed information report, and an annual financial report stating the salaries and expense account of union officers and of loans made by the union to officers or employees of the union. A member may obtain a copy of these forms from the Office of Labor-Management Standards Enforcement, U.S. Department of Labor, 200 Constitution Avenue, N.W., Washington, D.C. 20216.

The Landrum-Griffin Law limits the ability of a parent-union to impose a trusteeship on the local union for any reason, such as for alleged corruption or mismanagement of union funds, etc.

Section 401 of this law provides for secret ballot election of union officers. Local unions must elect officers at least once every three years. National or international unions must elect officers at least once every five years. Intermediate unions, such as joint boards, must elect officers at least once every four years. If a member wants to be a candidate for an office in his union, he is given certain rights to have a list of names and addresses of the members so that he may send his campaign propaganda to them. Members cannot be disqualified from running for a union office, or from voting in a union election for an unfair reason.

Another part of the Landrum-Griffin Act pro-

vides for certain safeguards of union funds, including that officers of the union be bonded.
Shop stewards, as well as officers or business
agents, must be bonded. For more information
about this law, you may contact the Office of
Labor-Management Standards Enforcement, U.S.
Department of Labor, 200 Constitution Avenue,
N.W., Washington, D.C. 20216, or an area or
regional office of this agency.

part six

Appendices

Appendices

Appendix A

Suggested readings

Listed below are some of the books or pamphlets you will find helpful if you want to learn more about labor relations. They are easy to read.

Clarence M. Updegroff. *Arbitration and Labor Relations*, 3d ed. Washington, D.C.: Bureau of National Affairs, Inc., 1970.

Basic Patterns in Union Contracts, 7th ed. Washington, D.C.: Bureau of National Affairs, Inc., About 52 pages, paperback.

Highlights of the New Pension Reform Law. Rockville, Ind.: Bureau of National Affairs, Inc. Paperback, 365 pages.

The Job Safety and Health Act of 1970. Washington, D.C.: Bureau of National Affairs, Inc., 1971. 342 pages.

Wesley M. Wilson. *Labor Law Handbook*. Indianapolis: Bobbs-Merrill Co., 1963. 518 pages plus cumulative pocket supplement, about 144 pages.

Wesley M. Wilson. *The Labor Relations Primer*. Homewood, Ill.: Dow Jones-Irwin, Inc., 106 pages.

The 1972 Civil Rights Law and Your Business. Englewood Cliffs, New Jersey: Prentice-Hall, Inc., Dept. S-L-CR-103, 1972. 48 pages, paperback.

The following booklets with paper covers are available from the Superintendent of Documents, U.S. Government Printing Office, Washington, D.C. 20402.

Brief History of the American Labor Movement, Catalog No. L2.3: 1000/4S/N 2901–0388 (1970).

Growth of Labor Law in the United States, Catalog No. L1.2:L 41/967, about 311 pages (1967).

Industrial Relations and Wage Terms, Bulletin No. 1438, U.S. Department of Labor, about 103 pages (1965).

Appendix B

Addresses of NLRB regional offices
Region

1. Boston, Mass. 02203, 7th Floor, Bullfinch Building, 15 New Chardon Street

2. New York, N.Y. 10022, 36th Floor, Federal Building, 26 Federal Plaza

3. Buffalo, NY 14202, 9th Floor, Federal Building, 111 W. Huron Street
   Albany, N.Y. 12207, New Federal Building, Clinton Avenue at North Pearl Street (Resident Office)

4. Philadelphia, Pa. 19106, William J. Green Federal Building, 600 Arch Street

5. Baltimore, Md. 21202, Federal Building, Room 1019, Charles Center

6. Pittsburgh, Pa. 15222, 1536 Federal Building, 1000 Liberty Avenue

7. Detroit, Mich. 48226, 500 Book Building, 1249 Washington Boulevard

8. Cleveland, O. 44199, 1695 Federal Office Building, 1240 East 9th Street

9.   Cincinnati, O. 45202, Federal Office Building, Room 3003, 550 Main Street.

10. Atlanta, Ga. 30328, 730 Peachtree Street, N.E., Room 701
     Birmingham, Ala. 35203, 2102 City Federal Building, 2026 Second Avenue North (Resident Office)

11. Winston-Salem, N.C. 27101, 16th Floor, Wachovia Building, 301 North Main Street.

12. Tampa, Fla. 33602, Room 706, Federal Office Building, 500 Zack Street.
     Jacksonville, Fla. 32202, Federal Building, 400 West Bay Street
     Miami, Fla. 33130, Room 826, Federal Office Building, 51 South West 1st Ave. (Resident Office)

13. Chicago, Ill. 60604, 881 Everett McKinley Dirksen Building, 219 South Dearborn Street.
     Peoria, Ill. 61602, 10th Floor, Savings Center Tower, 411 Hamilton Boulevard

14. St. Louis, Mo. 63101, Room 448, North 12th Boulevard.

15. New Orleans, 70113, Suite 2700, Plaza Tower, 1001 Howard Avenue

16. Fort Worth, Tex. 76102, Room 8A24, Federal Office Building, 819 Taylor St.

17. Kansas City, Kan. 66101, 616 Two Gateway Center, Fourth at State

18. Minneapolis, Minn. 55401, 316 Federal Building, 110 South 4th Street

19. Seattle, Wash. 98104, 29th Floor, Federal Building, 915 Second Ave.

Portland, Ore. 97205, 310 Six Ten Broadway Building, 610 South West Broadway Subregion 36)

20. San Francisco, Calif. 94102, 13050 Federal Building, 450 Golden Gate Avenue, Box 36047.

    Honolulu, Hawaii 96814, 1311 Kapiolani Boulevard, Suite 308 (Subregion 37)

21. Los Angeles, Calif. 90014, Eastern Columbia Building, 849 South Broadway

22. Newark, N.J. 07102, Federal Building, 16th Floor, 970 Broad Street

23. Houston, Tex. 77002, 4th Floor, Dallas Brazos Building, 1125 Brazos Street

24. Hato Rey, Puerto Rico 00919, 7th Floor, El Hato Rey Building, 255 Ponce de Leon Avenue

25. Indianapolis, Ind. 46204, Room 232, Federal Office Building, 575 North Pennsylvania Street

26. Memphis, Tenn. 38103, 746 Federal Office Building, 167 North Main Street

    Little Rock, Ark. 72201, 3511 Federal Building, 700 West Capital Avenue (Resident Office)

    Nashville, Tenn. 37203, Room A-702, Federal Courthouse Building, 801 Broadway (Resident Office)

27. Denver, Colo. 80202, New Custom House, Room 260, 721 19th Street

28. Phoenix, Ariz. 85014, LaTorre Building, 6107 North 7th Street

    Albuquerque, N.M. 87110, Patio Plaza

Building, 5000 Marble Ave. N.E. (Resident Office)

El Paso, Tex. 79901, Room 1025, The Mills Bldg., 303 North Oregon. (Resident Office)

29. Brooklyn, N.Y. 11241, 4th Floor, 16 Court Street

30. Milwaukee, Wisc. 53203, Second Floor, Commerce Building, 744 North 4th St.

31. Los Angeles, Calif. 90024, Federal Building, Room 12100, 11000 Wilshire Boulevard

Equal Employment Opportunities Commission offices

Headquarters

2400 Virginia Avenue, N.W., Washington, D.C.
20415

Regional Offices

New York, N.Y. 10007, Federal Office Building, Room 1615, 26 Federal Plaza

Philadelphia, Pa. 19106, 127 North Fourth Street.

Atlanta, Ga. 30303, Citizens Trust Building, 11th Floor, 75 Piedmont Avenue, N.E.

Chicago, Ill. 60605, 600 South Michigan Avenue, Room 611

Dallas, Tex. 75202, 1100 Commerce Street, Room 5A4

Kansas City, Mo. 64106, 601 East 12th Street, Room 113

San Francisco, Calif. 94104, 300 Montgomery Street, Suite 740

Sample ballot

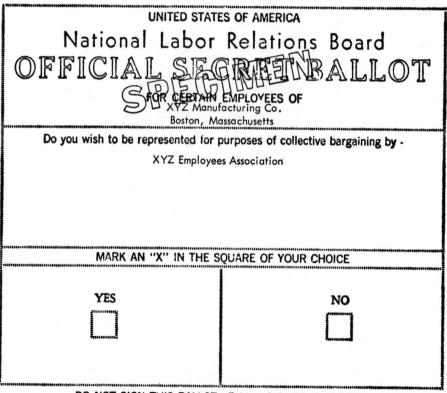

UNITED STATES OF AMERICA

National Labor Relations Board

OFFICIAL SECRET BALLOT

FOR CERTAIN EMPLOYEES OF
XYZ Manufacturing Co.
Boston, Massachusetts

Do you wish to be represented for purposes of collective bargaining by -

XYZ Employees Association

MARK AN "X" IN THE SQUARE OF YOUR CHOICE

YES	NO
☐	☐

DO NOT SIGN THIS BALLOT. Fold and drop in ballot box.
If you spoil this ballot return it to the Board Agent for a new one.

Appendix E

Authorization

I hereby designate and authorize the XYZ Employees Association as my collective bargaining agent in all matters pertaining to wages, hours, and other terms and conditions of employment.

_____	_____
Date	Signature
	_____
	Address
	_____
	City State Zip

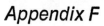

Petition for Decertification Election

Form NLRB–502 (11–64)	UNITED STATES OF AMERICA NATIONAL LABOR RELATIONS BOARD	Form Approved. Budget Bureau No. 64-R002.14

PETITION

	DO NOT WRITE IN THIS SPACE
	CASE NO

INSTRUCTIONS.—Submit an original and four (4) copies of this Petition to the NLRB Regional Office in the Region in which the employer concerned is located.
If more space is required for any one item, attach additional sheets, numbering item accordingly.

DATE FILED

The Petitioner alleges that the following circumstances exist and requests that the National Labor Relations Board proceed under its proper authority pursuant to Section 9 of the National Labor Relations Act.

1. Purpose of this Petition *(If box RC, RM, or RD is checked and a charge under Section 8(b)(7) of the Act has been filed involving the Employer named herein, the statement following the description of the type of petition shall not be deemed made.)*

(Check one)

☐ **RC–CERTIFICATION OF REPRESENTATIVES**—A substantial number of employees wish to be represented for purposes of collective bargaining by Petitioner and Petitioner desires to be certified as representative of the employees.

☐ **RM–REPRESENTATION (EMPLOYER PETITION)**—One or more individuals or labor organizations have presented a claim to Petitioner to be recognized as the representative of employees of Petitioner.

☒ **RD–DECERTIFICATION**—A substantial number of employees assert that the certified or currently recognized bargaining representative is no longer their representative.

☐ **UD–WITHDRAWAL OF UNION SHOP AUTHORITY**—Thirty percent (30%) or more of employees in a bargaining unit covered by an agreement between their employer and a labor organization desire that such authority be rescinded.

☐ **UC–UNIT CLARIFICATION**—A labor organization is currently recognized by employer, but petitioner seeks clarification of placement of certain employees: *(Check one)* ☐ In unit not previously certified

☐ In unit previously certified in Case No. _____

☐ **AC–AMENDMENT OF CERTIFICATION**—Petitioner seeks amendment of certification issued in Case No. _____

Attach statement describing the specific amendment sought.

2. NAME OF EMPLOYER	EMPLOYER REPRESENTATIVE TO CONTACT	PHONE NO
XYZ Manufacturing Co.	John Henry	222-2222

3. ADDRESS(ES) OF ESTABLISHMENT(S) INVOLVED *(Street and number, city, State, and ZIP Code)*

P.O. Box 100, Boston, Massachusetts

4a. TYPE OF ESTABLISHMENT *(Factory, mine, wholesaler, etc.)*	4b. IDENTIFY PRINCIPAL PRODUCT OR SERVICE
Manufacturing	Metal Specialties

5. Unit Involved *(In UC petition, describe PRESENT bargaining unit and attach description of proposed clarification.)*

	6a. NUMBER OF EMPLOYEES IN UNIT
Included All production and maintenance employees	PRESENT about 200
	PROPOSED (BY UC/AC)
Excluded Office clerical employees, professional employees, guards and/or watchmen, and supervisors as defined in the Act.	6b. IS THIS PETITION SUPPORTED BY 30% OR MORE OF THE EMPLOYEES IN THE UNIT?* ☒ YES ☐ NO *Not applicable in RM, UC, and AC

(If you have checked box RC in 1 above, check and complete EITHER item 7a or 7b, whichever is applicable)

7a. ☐ Request for recognition as Bargaining Representative was made on .... *(Month, day, year)* .... and Employer declined recognition on or about .... *(Month, day, year)* .... *(If no reply received, so state)*

7b. ☐ Petitioner is currently recognized as Bargaining Representative and desires certification under the act.

8. Recognized or Certified Bargaining Agent *(If there is none, so state)*

NAME	AFFILIATION
XYZ Employees Association	Independent
ADDRESS	DATE OF RECOGNITION OR CERTIFICATION
1000 East 100th Street, Boston, Massachusetts	January 28, 1972

9. DATE OF EXPIRATION OF CURRENT CONTRACT, IF ANY *(Show month, day, and year)*	10. IF YOU HAVE CHECKED BOX UD IN 1 ABOVE, SHOW HERE THE DATE OF EXECUTION OF AGREEMENT GRANTING UNION SHOP *(Month, day, and year)*
None	

11a. IS THERE NOW A STRIKE OR PICKETING AT THE EMPLOYER'S ESTABLISHMENT(S) INVOLVED? YES .... NO .. **X** .. | 11b. IF SO, APPROXIMATELY HOW MANY EMPLOYEES ARE PARTICIPATING?

11c. THE EMPLOYER HAS BEEN PICKETED BY OR ON BEHALF OF .... A LABOR *(Insert name)*

ORGANIZATION, OF .... *(Insert address)* .... SINCE .... *(Month, day, year)*

12. ORGANIZATIONS OR INDIVIDUALS OTHER THAN PETITIONER (AND OTHER THAN THOSE NAMED IN ITEMS 8 AND 11c), WHICH HAVE CLAIMED RECOGNITION AS REPRESENTATIVES AND OTHER ORGANIZATIONS AND INDIVIDUALS KNOWN TO HAVE A REPRESENTATIVE INTEREST IN ANY EMPLOYEES IN THE UNIT DESCRIBED IN ITEM 5 ABOVE. (IF NONE, SO STATE.)

NAME	AFFILIATION	ADDRESS	DATE OF CLAIM *(Required only if Petition is filed by Employer)*

I declare that I have read the above petition and that the statements therein are true to the best of my knowledge and belief.

Bill Smith

(Petitioner and affiliation, if any)

By s/Bill Smith .... An Individual

(Signature of representative or person filing petition) .... *(Title, if any)*

Address 101 East 10th Street, Boston, Massachusetts 123-4567

(Street and number, city, State, and ZIP Code) .... *(Telephone number)*

WILLFULLY FALSE STATEMENT ON THIS PETITION CAN BE PUNISHED BY FINE AND IMPRISONMENT (U.S. CODE, TITLE 18, SECTION 1001)

GPO 894-283

Petition for Certification of Representatives

Form NLRB–502 (11–64)	UNITED STATES OF AMERICA NATIONAL LABOR RELATIONS BOARD	Form Approved. Budget Bureau No. 64-R002.14

PETITION

DO NOT WRITE IN THIS SPACE

CASE NO.

INSTRUCTIONS.—Submit an original and four (4) copies of this Petition to the NLRB Regional Office in the Region in which the employer concerned is located.
If more space is required for any one item, attach additional sheets, numbering item accordingly.

DATE FILED

The Petitioner alleges that the following circumstances exist and requests that the National Labor Relations Board proceed under its proper authority pursuant to Section 9 of the National Labor Relations Act.

1. Purpose of this Petition *(If box RC, RM, or RD is checked and a charge under Section 8(b)(7) of the Act has been filed involving the Employer named herein, the statement following the description of the type of petition shall not be deemed made.)*

(Check one)

[X] **RC–CERTIFICATION OF REPRESENTATIVES**—A substantial number of employees wish to be represented for purposes of collective bargaining by Petitioner and Petitioner desires to be certified as representative of the employees.

[ ] **RM–REPRESENTATION (EMPLOYER PETITION)**—One or more individuals or labor organizations have presented a claim to Petitioner to be recognized as the representative of employees of Petitioner.

[ ] **RD–DECERTIFICATION**—A substantial number of employees assert that the certified or currently recognized bargaining representative is no longer their representative.

[ ] **UD–WITHDRAWAL OF UNION SHOP AUTHORITY**—Thirty percent (30%) or more of employees in a bargaining unit covered by an agreement between their employer and a labor organization desire that such authority be rescinded.

[ ] **UC–UNIT CLARIFICATION**—A labor organization is currently recognized by employer, but petitioner seeks clarification of placement of certain employees: *(Check one)* [ ] In unit not previously certified
[ ] In unit previously certified in Case No. _____

[ ] **AC–AMENDMENT OF CERTIFICATION**—Petitioner seeks amendment of certification issued in Case No. _____

Attach statement describing the specific amendment sought.

2. NAME OF EMPLOYER	EMPLOYER REPRESENTATIVE TO CONTACT	PHONE NO.
XYZ Manufacturing Co.	John Hancock	222-2222

3. ADDRESS(ES) OF ESTABLISHMENT(S) INVOLVED *(Street and number, city, State, and ZIP Code)*

P.O. Box 100, Boston, Massachusetts

4a. TYPE OF ESTABLISHMENT *(Factory, mine, wholesaler, etc.)*	4b. IDENTIFY PRINCIPAL PRODUCT OR SERVICE
Manufacturing	Metal Specialties

5. Unit Involved *(In UC petition, describe PRESENT bargaining unit and attach description of proposed clarification.)*

6a. NUMBER OF EMPLOYEES IN UNIT.

Included

All production and maintenance employees

PRESENT about 200

PROPOSED (BY UC/AC)

Excluded

Office clerical employees, professional employees, guards and/or watchmen, and supervisors as defined in the Act.

6b. IS THIS PETITION SUPPORTED BY 30% OR MORE OF THE EMPLOYEES IN THE UNIT?
[X] YES [ ] NO
*Not applicable in RM, UC, and AC

(If you have checked box RC in 1 above, check and complete EITHER item 7a or 7b, whichever is applicable)

7a. [ ] Request for recognition as Bargaining Representative was made on .... *(Month, day, year)* ....and Employer

declined recognition on or about .... *(Month, day, year)* .... *(If no reply received, so state)*

7b. [ ] Petitioner is currently recognized as Bargaining Representative and desires certification under the act.

8. Recognized or Certified Bargaining Agent *(If there is none, so state)*

NAME	AFFILIATION
None	
ADDRESS	DATE OF RECOGNITION OR CERTIFICATION

9. DATE OF EXPIRATION OF CURRENT CONTRACT, IF ANY *(Show month, day, and year)*	10. IF YOU HAVE CHECKED BOX UD IN 1 ABOVE, SHOW HERE THE DATE OF EXECUTION OF AGREEMENT GRANTING UNION SHOP *(Month, day, and year)*
None	

11a. IS THERE NOW A STRIKE OR PICKETING AT THE EMPLOYER'S ESTABLISHMENT(S) INVOLVED? YES .... NO ...X....	11b. IF SO, APPROXIMATELY HOW MANY EMPLOYEES ARE PARTICIPATING?

11c. THE EMPLOYER HAS BEEN PICKETED BY OR ON BEHALF OF .... *(Insert name)* .... A LABOR

ORGANIZATION, OF .... *(Insert address)* .... SINCE .... *(Month, day, year)*

12. ORGANIZATIONS OR INDIVIDUALS OTHER THAN PETITIONER (AND OTHER THAN THOSE NAMED IN ITEMS 8 AND 11c), WHICH HAVE CLAIMED RECOGNITION AS REPRESENTATIVES AND OTHER ORGANIZATIONS AND INDIVIDUALS KNOWN TO HAVE A REPRESENTATIVE INTEREST IN ANY EMPLOYEES IN THE UNIT DESCRIBED IN ITEM 5 ABOVE (IF NONE, SO STATE.)

NAME	AFFILIATION	ADDRESS	DATE OF CLAIM *(Required only if Petition is filed by Employer)*

I declare that I have read the above petition and that the statements therein are true to the best of my knowledge and belief.

XYZ Employees Association
(Petitioner and affiliation, if any)

By s/John Doe
(Signature of representative or person filing petition)

An Individual
(Title, if any)

Address 1000 East 100th Street, Boston, Massachusetts
(Street and number, city, State, and ZIP Code)

333-3333
(Telephone number)

WILLFULLY FALSE STATEMENT ON THIS PETITION CAN BE PUNISHED BY FINE AND IMPRISONMENT (U.S. CODE, TITLE 18, SECTION 1001)

GPO 894-283

Index

A

Ads, newspaper, 2
Affirmative action plans, 12
Age, discrimination because of, 13
Agency shop, 96
Agreements for NLRB election, 84
Agricultural laborers, 4
Antidiscrimination laws, 6–17, 35–40, 122–25
Applying for a job, 1
Appropriate bargaining unit, 75
Arbitration, 101
Assistance of union by employer, 137

B

Bargaining unit for union, 75
Benefit plans, 48–57
Business necessity as a defense to discrimination charges, 37

C

Certification of union by NLRB, 92
Challenged ballots, 90
Charges, filing, antidiscrimination, 7–9
  NLRB, unfair labor practice, 135
Checkoff of union dues, 97
Child labor, 24
Clothing, special, required, 27
Coercion of employees
  by employers, 136
  by unions, 142

Coercion by unions, to force recognition, 153
Collections, wages, laws relating to, 29
Common law of the shop, 42
Complaints, presenting to employer, 31
Consolidations of employers, 129

D

Day of rest laws, 24
Decertification elections, 81
  petition form, 180
Decision of NLRB regional director for elections, 85
Deductions from pay, statement of, 27
Dental insurance, 52
Discrimination
  because of
    age, 13, 122
    color, 36, 122
    handicap, 39
    race, 36, 122
    religion, 37, 123
    sex, 36, 122
  by employers because of union activity, 138
  by unions, 131, 146
Discussing job performance with your boss, 40
Dues checkoff, 97

185